T0107093

ONE WITH OTHERS
[a little book of her days]

BOOKS BY C.D. WRIGHT

One With Others [*a little book of her days*]

Rising, Falling, Hovering

One Big Self: An Investigation

Like Something Flying Backwards: New and Selected Poems

Cooling Time: An American Poetry Vigil

One Big Self: Prisoners of Louisiana,
    photographs by Deborah Luster, with text by C.D. Wright

Steal Away: Selected and New Poems

Deepstep Come Shining

Tremble

The Lost Roads Project: A Walk-in Book of Arkansas,
    with photographs by Deborah Luster

Just Whistle: a valentine,
    with photographs by Deborah Luster

String Light

Further Adventures with You

Translations of the Gospel Back into Tongues

C.D. WRIGHT

ONE
WITH
OTHERS

[a little book of her days]

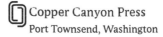 Copper Canyon Press
Port Townsend, Washington

Copyright 2010 by C.D. Wright

All rights reserved

Printed in the United States of America

Cover art: Deborah Luster, "Pump House, Forrest City, Arkansas," 2006.

Copper Canyon Press is in residence at Fort Worden State Park in Port Townsend, Washington, under the auspices of Centrum. Centrum is a gathering place for artists and creative thinkers from around the world, students of all ages and backgrounds, and audiences seeking extraordinary cultural enrichment.

LIBRARY OF CONGRESS CATALOGING-IN-PUBLICATION DATA

Wright, C.D.
One with others : a little book of her days / C.D. Wright.
    p. cm.
ISBN 978-1-55659-324-6 (alk. paper)
1. Civil rights movements—Poetry. 2. Civil rights movements—
Arkansas—History—20th century. I. Title.
PS3573.R497O58 2010
811´.54—dc22

                                                    2010016789

ISBN 978-1-55659-388-8 (paperback)

COPPER CANYON PRESS
Post Office Box 271
Port Townsend, Washington 98368
WWW.COPPERCANYONPRESS.ORG

I want people of twenty seven languages walking back and forth saying to one another hello brother how's the fishing
and when they reach their destination I don't want them to forget if it was bad

—*The Battlefield Where the Moon Says I Love You,* Frank Stanford

There are people in small rooms all over the world, in impersonal cubicles in large offices, in malls, in ghettos, and behind fenced mansions—who thrive on a little chaos, enjoy the occasional taste of 220 volts, live for the beauty of the flaw in the grain.

—*It Came from Memphis,* Robert Gordon

No, I do not weep at the world—I am too busy sharpening my oyster knife.

—"How It Feels to Be Colored Me," Zora Neale Hurston

Herein lie buried many things.

—*The Souls of Black Folk,* W.E.B. DuBois

ONE WITH OTHERS
[a little book of her days]

Some names were changed or omitted in light of the interpretive nature of this account. Others because they still live there. People may have been rendered as semblances and composites of one another. And others, spoken into being. Memories have been tapped, and newspapers consulted. Books referenced. Times fused and towns overlaid. This is not a work of history. It is a report full of holes, a little commemorative edition, and it aspires to the borrowed-tuxedo lining of fiction. In the end, it is a welter of associations.

Up and down the towns in the Delta, people were stirring. Cotton was right about shoe top. Day lilies hung from their withering necks. Temperatures started out in the 90s with no promise of a good soaking. School was almost out. The farm bells slowly rang for freedom. The King lay moldering in the ground over a year. The scent of liberation stayed on, but it was hard to bring the trophy home. Hard to know what came next; one thing, and one thing only was known, no one wanted to go home dragging their tow sack; no one wanted to go home empty-handed.

Over at the all-Negro junior high, a popular teacher has been fired for "insubordination" for a "derogatory" letter he wrote the superintendent saying the Negro has no voice. No voice at all. It was the start of another cacophonous summer.

It smells like home. She said, dying. And I, What's that you smell, V. And V, dying: The faint cut of walnuts in the grass. My husband's work shirt on the railing. The pulled-barbecued evening. The turned dirt. Even in this pitch I can see the vapor-lit pole, the crape myrtle not in shadow. My sweet-betsy. That exact streaked sky. The mongrel dog being pelted with rain. Mine eyes pelted. All fear. Overcome. At last. No scent. That's what she said. Dying in the one-room apartment in Hell's Kitchen.

MR. EASTER, AN OUTLIER [with FISH 4 SALE]: It's probably a rat snake. Had a couple in the old storm cellar. My son-in-law accidentally caught it on fire and it killed ever one of my snakes.

✝ ✝ ✝

I came in by the old road from Memphis, the old military road. Across the iron bridge. No one in the field. Not a living soul.

I drove around with the windows down. The redbuds in bloom. Sky, a discolored chenille spread. Weather, generally fair.

The marchers step off from the jailhouse at Bragg's Spur, 8:17 a.m. More police than reporters. More reporters than police.

The self-described Prime Minister of the Invaders, 31, and five others have begun their trek. SWEET WILLIE WINE'S WALK AGAINST FEAR is on the move.

V: We had the water and the shoes in my car. There was a black man named Stiles. [He was a midget.] He kept that water good and cold [for the marchers].

The threat they say is coming from the east [of the six Negroes walking to Little Rock and the white woman driving a station wagon].

It was something you came through that.

V: It was invigorating. It was the most alive I ever felt in my life.

FBI followed me for a long time. Stringers for the *Gazette* and the *Appeal* trailed me for a year. Once every ten or twelve years, I will get a caller. I used all of my life. I told my friend Gert, you've got your life until you use it.

I park in a spot of shade and walk around.

Downtown half shut down.

Cotton gin still going, not strong, but going.

Tracks working, neglected, but working.

The infamous overpass brought down.

September 15, 2004, Hell's Kitchen, her life surrendered to her body. September 15 the day Padre Hidalgo uttered the famous *Grito* that kicked off the Mexican Revolution. She would have liked that, going off the air on a day marking a great struggle for independence.

The river rises from a mountain of granite.

The river receives the water of the little river.

The house where my friend once lived, indefinitely empty.

Walnuts turning dark in the grass. Papers collected on the porch.

If I put my face to the glass, I can make out the ghost

of her ironing board, bottle of bourbon on the end.

✛ ✛ ✛

HER FORMER HUSBAND: I'd come home from work and she would be in a rage and I just couldn't understand it.

They were a poor match. He says so to this day. She said so then. They barely tolerated one another. But they were Catholic [another "error bred in the bone"]. If he looked at her, and she looked at him, in nine months she was back at the lying-in.

[My best guess: She woke up in a rage, eight days a week.]

Her friends—the musician, the poet, the actor:
GERT: She taught me how to live. Now she has taught me how to die.

And I: She was my goombah. My *rafiki.* It was the honor of my life to know her. Honor of my life.

ELLIS:

A crowd/ Will gather, and not know it walks the very street

Whereon a thing once walked that seemed a burning cloud.

[Yeats she knew inside out. Inside out.]

A MAN KNOWN AS SKEETER [his whole life]: Oh yeah, I remember her, she celebrated all her kids' birthdays on the same day.

I talked to a number of people. In person. On the phone. Mostly, the phone. When I could get anyone to talk to me. I made so many calls:

Can we talk later because I'm trying to cook for my family

He's not here now

He's fishing

I've got to go to the hospital to see my brother

He's about to pass

I've got to go to Memphis

I've got to work the night shift

Out at the big pen

I work there since the plant shut

Can we talk later

I'm on Neighborhood Watch

And the kids are walking out

There's no food here

I'm left holding the baby

You'll have to speak to the hand

This was my rest day

He's fishing

I'm working at the polls I'm on poll watch

I've got to go to Little Rock for my checkup

My pressure's gone up

Since he got laid off

He's always fishing

When he can't go he's home watching

The fishing channel

So, how is the fishing

Oh well, you know

It's lots worse elsewhere

The woman who lived next door to the old house came outside to pick up her paper. I asked if she had known my friend V who lived there in the 1960s, and she allowed that she did.

Flat out she says, She didn't trust me and I didn't trust her.

Then she surprised me, saying, She was right. We were wrong.

[I heard just a fraction of the terrible things that happened back then. A fraction.]

Then she shocked me, saying, They have souls just like us.

I see my friend, midthirties, waking up in stifling heat. Her seven towheaded children balled up in their dreams. Socks and shorts dropped across scuffed-up floors. The funk of high-tops bonding with the wallpaper.

She wakes up seething but eases the screen door to. I see my friend breaking a stem off the bush at the side of the house and breathe in, sweet-betsy. She nudges a slug with her toe.

MR. EASTER: I'm about like you though about a snake. All these years on the river I only saw a poison one about three times.

The chaplain for the state police brings up the rear in his own car with refreshments for the men.

The only sure thing were the prices [and the temperatures]:

2 pounds of Oleo costs 25¢.

And 5 cans of Cherokee freestone peaches are $1.

The Cosmos Club president held a tea at her lovely lakeside home.

Two more Big Tree boys make fine soldiers.

A Rolling Stone was found in the bottom of his swimming pool.

Rufus Thomas and his Bear Cats will headline at the Negro Fair.

And Miss Teenage Arkansas [a comely young miss] is saluted once again

for her charm and pulchritude.

Sunshine fresh Hydrox cookies, 1 lb for 59¢.

The assistant warden, at 300 pounds, is the one identified for administering the

strap at the Arkansas pen [a self-sustaining institution]. Several say they were

beaten for failing [to meet cotton quotas]. Others more often than not did not

know why [they were beaten]. One testified to more than 70 [beatings].

The strap is not in question. In question is when it is to be administered.

THE VERY REVEREND PILLOW [at Bedside Baptist]: The injury that

the rock-hard lie of inequality performs is unspeakable; it is irremediable, can

be insurmountable. And very very thorough. No peculiar feeling to the contrary

can be permitted to gain hold. You get my meaning.

Back then, in case of rain, I would be lying if I did not say to you—you
would be ill-advised to step under the generous eave of certain stores or [in
the unforgiving heat] to take a drink from a cooler or even try to order catfish
[at Saturday's]. And don't even think about applying for the soda jerk job [at
Harmon's] or playing dominoes [at the Legion Hut].

Back then we could not be having this conversation. You get what I'm
getting at.

Back then I would not be at this end of town unless I was pushing a mower
or a wheelbarrow, the teacher [retired] told me over a big Coke at the Colonel's;
even at that, back then, I would not be here, if the sun was headed down.

[How far did a man have to walk just to pass his water, back then?]

The river is impounded by
the lake; below the lake the river
enters the lowlands, it slithers
through cypress and willow. And the air
itself, cloudy or clear, stirring

with smoke or dust or malathion,

if you get my drift, must not

be construed to be indivisible. No more

than blood. There is black blood

and white blood. There is black air

and white air; this includes

the air in the tires blowing out

over the interstate between town and

river, the air that riddles the children

when a crop duster buzzes

a schoolyard, the air that bellows

from the choir of robes

when the Very Reverend Pillow

bids, Be seated, and even the air socked

from the jaw of the champ, born

seventeen miles west, in Sand Slough,

when he took that phantom punch

the year in which this particular round

of troubles began.

Today, Gentle Reader,

the sermon once again: "Segregation

After Death." *Showers in the a.m.*

The threat they say is moving from the east.

The sheriff's club says Not now. Not

nokindofhow. Not never. The children's

minds say Never waver. Air

fanned by a flock of hands in the old

funeral home where the meetings

were called [because Mrs. Oliver

owned it free and clear], and

that selfsame air, sanctified

and doomed, rent with racism, and

it percolates up from the soil itself,

which in these parts is richer than Elvis,

and up on the Ridge is called loess

[pronounced "luss"], off-color, windblown stuff.

This is where Hemingway penned some

of *A Farewell to Arms,* on the Ridge

[when he was married to Pauline]. Where

the mayor of Memphis moved after

his ill-starred term. After they slew

the dreamer and began to slay

the dream. Once an undulant kingdom

of Elberta and Early Wheeler peaches.

Hot air chopping

through clods of earth with

each stroke of the tenant

boy's hoe [Dyess Colony] back

when the boy hadn't an iota

of becoming the Man in Black.

Al Green hailed from here;

Sonny Liston, 12th of 13 kids,

[some say 24th of 25]

born 17 miles west,

in Sand Slough. Head hardened

on hickory sticks. [And Scott Bond,

born a slave, became a millionaire.

Bought a drove of farms

around Big Tree. Planted potatoes.

When the price came back up,

planted cotton. Bought gravel. Felled

his own timber. A buy-and-sell individual.

When you look close at his picture, you

can't tell if he was white

or black. You can just tell he was a trim,

cross-eyed fellow.] And the Silver Fox,

he started out in Colt.

Mostly up-and-down kind of men.

[Except for Mr. Bond, he went in one

direction when it came around

to making money.]

✝ ✝ ✝

GRADUATE OF THE ALL-NEGRO SCHOOL: Our teacher would tell us, Turn to page 51. That page wouldn't be there.

GRADUATE OF THE ALL-WHITE SCHOOL, first year of Integration-By-Choice: Spent a year in classes by myself. They had spotters on the trampoline. I knew they would not spot me. You timed your trips to the restroom.

+ + +

She woke up in a housebound rage, my friend V. Changed diapers. Played poker. Drank bourbon. Played duplicate bridge. Made casseroles, grape salad, macaroni and cheese. Played cards with the priest. Made an argument for school uniforms, but the parents were concerned the children would be indistinguishable. She was thinking: affordable, uniforms. You can distinguish them, she argued, by their shoes. It was a mind on fire, a body confined.

And on the other side of Division, a whole other population in year-round lockdown.

A girl that knew all Dante once

Live[d] to bear children to a dunce.

[Yeats she knew well enough to wield as a weapon. It would pop out when she was put out. Over the ironing board. Over cards. Some years the Big Tree Catholic foursome would all be pregnant at once, playing bridge, their cards propped up on distended stomachs. Laughing their bourbon-logged heads off.]

She had a brain like the Reading Room in the old British Museum. She could have donned fingerless gloves and written *Das Kapital* while hexagons of snowflakes tumbled by the windowpanes. She could have made it up whole cloth. She could have sewn the cotton out of her own life. While the Thames froze over.

She loved: Words. Cats. Long-playing records. Laughter. Men.

Alcohol. Cigarettes. The supernatural. It makes for a carnal list. Pointless to rank. Five in diapers at once—a stench, she claimed, she never got used to.

+ + +

AMONG HER EFFECTS, a bourboned-up letter:

Dear Callie,

This grandmother of yours is an intoxicant and you are not. It makes me proud that you study calculus.

Euclid alone has looked on Beauty bare.

Anyway, there is one thing that happened that I want you to know about. One Arkansas summer, the summer of 1967? The boys came running in the house and said they saw an accident and we all ran down the road and there was this old man walking around in a daze and I asked if I could help him. There was a car in the ditch and Rudy and Will, I think, said no one was in it. The man said his name, which I forget, and asked me to call Mrs. Hand [an aristocrat with an elevator in her house] and ask her to send help.

I did. She took the message, thanked me and hung up.

About a month later, her son, a prominent town attorney, called me up and asked me to be a witness, and I told him that I hadn't seen anything. And he said, Come to court anyway. So I went.

The prosecutor, the D.A., was a man named Hunter Crumb. So I'm sitting in the witness chair, telling what happened and I referred to the dazed man, and I quote myself:

And that gentleman, I'm sorry, I have forgotten his name, came up to me and asked me to call Mrs. Hand.

Okay, I do not exaggerate, the D.A. got red in the face and said, "Did you call that [N-word] a gentleman?" and went on at length yelling at me. Face on fire, yelling. I looked at the judge. I looked at Mr. Hand, but they would not look at me. Finally I was allowed to step down. I was shocked.

The second thing I want you to know is that in mid-June of 1969, Sweet Willie Wine [aka, the Man Imported from Memphis or the Prime Minister or the Invader] and Mrs. Oliver called on Hunter Crumb, to present the proper permits for the boycott and ten minutes after they left that man's office Hunter

Crumb dropped dead of a heart attack. I don't have the news accounts of that,

but it happened, and it was like electricity in Big Tree.

    After that, I would have followed Sweet Willie Wine into hell.

✝ ✝ ✝

It gradually turns from clear to coffee;

the river receives another river near its mouth

and joins the mighty river to the south of Helena.

Yoncopin are the lilies in the ditches [pretty bloom

for a filthy drainage ditch isn't it now]. An Arkansas arc

is not a rainbow but an old iron bridge over troubled

brown waters. The cornea's collection of the earliest

rays ordering an entirely different distribution

of light and shade, I could imagine my friend V:

being blind and seeing everything, marrying a dozen

men and living alone, having seven children and

being barren, toting an M16 that looked

like a hoe, whistling down a taxi in a cold

capital; I could see the faded and ragged fields

replaced by blue shadows on hills of snow or

turning from a stag at the edge of the interstate

into a freshwater pearl before more sediment

entered the river than flowed from its mouth.

[Ninety-nine times out of a hundred, it's a rat snake.]

+ + +

Correction Facility Area

No Stopping

Stay Away

Stay Away

Remain Calm

You Watch

How You

Carry Yourself

I Told My Babies

My Beauties

And Don't You Go

Getting In That Line

Don't You Dare Go

Getting In That Line

Festina Lente

My Darlings,

Never Waver,

My Dears.

No more than blood:

There is black blood and white blood. There is black air and white air. And

this selfsame lie takes aim, even if by indirection, at the stifled lives of those

inflicting the harm, the lives of witting and of unwitting ignorance, and those

who must live among the stiflers, as if one of them, by all outward and visible

signs one of them, but on the reverse side of their skin lie awake in the scratchy dark, burning to cross over. Not to become one of the harmed but to shed the

skin, you get my meaning, the tainted skin of the injuring party.

Just *to act,* was the glorious thing.

And those so grievously harmed, who do the forgiving, do so, that they not

be deformed by the lie, must call on reserves not meant to be tapped except for

a once-in-a-lifetime crisis, a sudden death or what disclaimers call Acts-of-the-

Almighty such as a twister tearing over the land on which a plain frame house

stands, or if, in town, it will be of cinderblock, a yard of raked dirt, a stand of day

lilies, their withering heads lopped off.

But in this case, the reserves are needed every day, every hour of every

day, because the warp is everywhere, because one is supposed to look at one's

reflection and see an inferior, uncomely, unwantable thing, because those are

the terms for living, that is the conditioning. It is in fact, the law.

And a most elaborate system has been built up to ensure that the manchild

and the womanchild see a lesser face than the one that is there. It requires the

long crooked arm of enforcement, the duplication of services and facilities, with one set being far superior to the other set, which of course does not even aim to duplicate, but underscores the shoddiness of the second set of services and facilities, that they be "deservedly," emphatically unequal.

So, you will find the answers on page 51; though the answers are etched in bloodied ink on paper that has been torn out by your tormentors and dragged into a crawdad hole. Being a measure of society's distortion, in truth, the answers could have provided little inspiration for the rest of your life. Rather, their absence provides the inspiration, as a pop bottle flies toward a lightbulb and the Savoys commence stomping in the basement.

It also entails the complicity of the leaders of the faithful who are obliged to advance this doctrine as the Word of the Almighty, some of whom probably are believers in this malevolent reading, while others sign on for efficacy's sake and others by dint of intimidation.

And it enjoins the participation of merchants and professionals, and law enforcers and the extralegal forces of men known as Whitecappers, Night Riders, Klansmen, and Birchers [the latter termed by its local spokesman to be strictly an educational society dedicated to the defeat of communism];

men who openly congregate at a service station owned by the deputy or a city

barbershop or outbuilding of a big farm to conspire and collaborate or call

themselves Concerned Citizens and so can assemble in public buildings or even

the Legion Hut, the swell green slope of which has been used as a setting for

a cross in flames, facing the road, you see where I'm coming from, public and

semipublic places from which more than half the population is blatantly barred.

DEAR ABBY,

When Daryl and I were first married, he asked me to IRON his

undershorts. His mother always did. At first I didn't mind because we had no

children, but now have two, and I could save a lot of time tossing them in the

dryer and folding them, but I tried that once and I never heard the end of it.

Daryl says he could "feel" the difference. What would you do?

DEAR TOO MUCH IRONING,

I would iron his underwear. You are wasting more energy complaining and

arguing than it takes to iron seven pair of shorts once a week.

Everybody has a problem. What's yours.

+ + +

When I show the granddaughter of my friend's babysitter a picture of the

swimming pool taken when it was built in 1935, printed in a special promotional

edition of the paper to entice [white] people to move to the Jewel of the Delta,

her eyes flash/ fill/ clear:

We were not allowed to swim there/ We had never seen the dressing rooms/ We had never been near the locker room/ We had never seen the lights on their playing field except from the other side of Division.

✝ ✝ ✝

In Big Tree

People are reading their Bibles in bed

Their laces hang by their walking shoes

People are dreaming money semen

And boll weevils on the creep

Some could be soothed by a mourning dove

Some would be soothed by the Prince of Peace

UNDERTAKER: The night a threat wrapped in a brick came through that window, my mother, a mortician herself, said, Girl, forget calling the sheriff. Get the dustpan.

Some people want to lift you up and some are like a crawdad, they just want to drag you down.

[And there are those among the injured who cannot forgive the harm done because they have borne it since they opened their eyes, since the moment their perfectly good-seeing eyes made contact with the delusional eyes of their fellow citizens and lived to see this ignominy passed on; they cannot because the injury is inherently repugnant and because it feeds on a lie that appears to be alive and marked for service into perpetuity; so that not only must they endure its consequences, but so must their flesh, their blood, their firstborn.]

[Thus, the practice begins before the period of quickening before the crochet needle and catheter can be employed to prevent the quickening.]

[Where was it you wanted to bury this hatchet. Your land or mine.]

+ + +

V's bush was sweet-betsy. I broke off a twig in her oldest daughter's yard.

Over the coming months, I break it over and over for a quick hit of camphor.

And offshore Camille brought rain that September. The year they put the

kids under arrest and put them in the swimming pool.

King called "it" a disease, segregation. [Sounds contagious.]

It's cradle work is what it is. It begins before the quickening.

When V ended up back in Kentucky after her expulsion from Big Tree, she

kept a retired fighting cock. It was her only pleasure, Helmet. No one else could

get near him.

Long before this black and white issue, she said she was going to make up a

coat of arms and the motto on its heater would read:

I never knew what misery was till I came to Arkansas

Why wake up in this torpor—unless you happen to be from here. Which requires less than volition. It requires only inertia.

Or blood ties, where everyone you ever knew or were kin to lies buried.

Or, the long-lingering olfaction of home, whether from the faint cut of walnuts spoiled in the grass or a sour work shirt on a rotted railing. When the ones who are from here come home in the evening and get out of their car, and rise on tired legs, the barbecued night they smell is theirs—that exact streaked sky, that turned dirt, that crape myrtle, that dog chained to the clothesline.

✝ ✝ ✝

Love then, she was all but dying for, except the love of Catholic men, who did not live to love [from whom it was an article of faith that life is and forever shall be, for suffering].

V liked to say: It makes martyrs of the women and emasculates the men.

If religion, she also liked to say, is the opiate of the masses, fundamentalism is the amphetamine.

[That busted us up.]

The hierarchy, indisputable. The hereafter, actual. Sin, she believed in. That she was born in and bound to do it; she was likewise accepting of being sinned against. Injustice she rejected. Through and through.

Something else—LIE, was not in her vocabulary. The pure inflammatory truth she could take it, and Gentle Reader, she knew how to inflict it.

The night the town erupted, the night they beat the Memphis organizer, the Man Imported from Memphis, the City of Good Abode, the self-named Invader [the tag was picked from a sci-fi show; it stuck, and it sent its message straight to the eighth nerve].

The night they put some of the strangers in jail [in Swahili, stranger is *mgeni.* It also means "guest." Hereabouts, it means outside agitator; it means godless communist; it means Invader], a crazed white woman turned her hose on V and the Invaders through the bars, and a mad white mob set her car ablaze [the only car she would ever have];

and a little twig of a white kid went to the Bijou with his father.

The reel had just sputtered into action when the lady left the projection booth and ran down the aisle to the boy and his father. You've got to get out of here, this town's about to blow. And it was rare to go to a movie, rare for his daddy to take him, and he did not want to leave, he wanted to see the show, he wanted to see, but the lady had already stopped the projector and everyone else had cleared out.

It was all black. It was all white. It was black and white. No, it was in living color.

What was playing.
VETERINARIAN: You got me there.

You tend big animals or cats and dogs.

I'm small, I just take care of the small. If a heifer or a mare rolled over on me, that'd be all she wrote. I wouldn't be able to work anymore. So, I stick to small. My father treated every one of her cats, the Persians, the blue point Siamese. Long before the black and white issue. He knew them all.

Two of their descendants made it to Hell's Kitchen. They were ill-tempered, overweight, and generally obnoxious.

So, who would you rather live with, V asked, Al Capone or Mahatma Gandhi.

You got me there.

GRADUATE OF THE ALL-NEGRO HIGH SCHOOL: I did not participate [in the uprising]. I was in the band room, practicing. Keeping time. Our mother was very strict.

What was your band called.

Come again.

Your band.

You got me there.

GRADUATE OF THE ALL-WHITE HIGH SCHOOL, first year of

Integration-By-Choice: I did not participate. I was in the theater, practicing.

I was a smart kid, and I sort of knew I was going to leave, and that high

school was just something you had to go through to get to the rest of your life.

ALL-NEGRO HIGH SCHOOL ANNUAL:

Best Dancer: one of the boys beaten by the Night Riders

Biggest Wolf: son of one of the boys blinded by the Night Riders

Friendliest: his brother who jumped from the overpass

Best Running Back: his cousin, went pro [in Canada]

Smartest: her cousin had his own car—he drove her to Ohio still wearing

her cap and gown

Atmospheric washes of sound

Play it muddy

Play it freaking loud

Light sputtering and crackling

The only sure thing in those days were the prices:

Jack Sprat tea bags only 19¢.

A whole fryer is 59¢.

A half-gallon of Purex, 25¢.

Two pounds of Oleo, 25¢.

Ivory Soap 10¢ a bar.

Cherokee freestone peaches, 5 cans for $1.

And the temperatures:

Los Angeles enters its sixth day of rioting, 32 dead; Chicago's

rebellion ends in two.

KKK's lawyer dies in Birmingham.

Hurricane Camille sacks Pass Christian.

The president of the Cosmos Club holds a tea.

Soybean cyst nematode puts the county's crop under quarantine.

Three Brinkley children die in an icebox.

It is time to pick the cotton.

Come see, come touch this Frigidaire, this two-door wonder.

B-r-r-r-r.

It is not for you to see, not for you to touch [N-word].

G-r-r-r-r.

Elsewhere in the news, troths have been plithed to thee

and thee and thou and thine.

Nothing happens without mayonnaise.

An elusive local Negro is found in Chicago.

The difference in the sexes is liked by most people.

Two trains derail.

A $33,000 blanket bond is posted by three Negro farmers

for the children put in the pool.

GRADUATE OF THE ALL-WHITE HIGH SCHOOL, first year of

Integration-By-Choice: No homecoming games. There were two or three of us on

the team but we could not be in the stands.

Things we were unsure about, we found out to be true. We had new books at the all-white school, and the books they no longer used went to the all-Negro school.

If a teacher was overly nice to me, it came back on them.

Girls who had been state champs couldn't make the team. I was a cheerleader. I couldn't make the squad. Never went near a dance. Or the pool. Or the bowling alley. Could only go to the movies on Monday.

RADIO MINISTRY: Every chosen one of us is guilty as sin and sin is on everything a sinner ever touched from toilet seat to doorknob to gavel to gunlock. Now get in that goddamn water and swim with the rest of them. [I must have misheard him.]

The Savoys.

Come again.

My band. We were the Savoys.

HER FRIEND BIRDIE: We couldn't wait to go to V's house in the afternoon. Dell would call and say, Let's go to V's, and I would say, I've got to yadayadayada, and Dell would say, Just squirt some furniture polish in the air and Joey will think you've been cleaning all afternoon.

The first time I met her she told me about her goldfish committing suicide.

She showed me a picture of her daddy. How old do you think he is in this picture. Hah, she said, he was an alcoholic and he was only 58 years old.

She would have on Enrico Caruso and Nina Simone and Segovia, Bach and Leonard Cohen and Joan Baez and the Man in Black, all on the same stack. We had a whole education in fine arts and literature in her living room.

You've got to read this and you've got to read that. She had a lending library going on. You're not ready for James Joyce she told me and I never did read James Joyce. I just accepted it. We went big into T.S. Eliot; so I knew all about *Cats* before it ever got to Broadway. We listened to *A Child's Christmas in Wales* every year. Dell and her husband, Joey, made it over to Wales and laid a rose on the drunkard's stone.

She could have been a master teacher, but she said, No, she couldn't. She said she had nothing but contempt for her teacher when she discovered she didn't know Swinburne.

[One ought to admit V could rise in record time to the condition of contempt.]

HER FRIEND THE ACTOR: She once got on a wrathful tear about a particular member of Congress, or some churlish priest, and ended up on her feet in a lively enactment of how she would like to saw that MF in half. Left-handed. [I guess an untidy job of it would hurt a lot more.]

She kept her Saigon cinnamon in her purse so the fifth boychild couldn't get his hands on it.

Dragged her sewing machine to her porch because she did not want to have to look at it.

When she had cancer, after the last child was born, and had a hysterectomy, she didn't want anyone to know. She didn't want them saying, That poor woman with all those children and now she's got cancer.

The movie was *Run Wild, Run Free.*

Come again.

Also known as *The White Colt.* A little mute boy roams the moors alone.

Wouldn't you like to run wild, run free, roam the moors. Meet an albino pony.

A kind colonel. A girl your age. A pet falcon. Wouldn't you like to rescue the

blue-eyed horse. Especially if it returned to you your long-suppressed voice.

For the reading kids from the low-lying fields of Arkansas, the very term *moors*

projected a mythic land where [white] children ran wild and free. The other

Moors, no one ever dreamed of such a people. They were inconceivable. Nor did

the Renaissance reach the western shore of the Mississippi.

She completed the circle of this life in Hell's Kitchen

The attending doctor lived upstairs

He and his partner nailed a small brass plaque

To the barren pear outside her window

Her name, date of birth, date of death

The mule train march has been canceled

The preachers are staying home

The March Against Fear is on

The Man Imported from Memphis is walking

The combines are moving into position

LOCAL MAN: I was going to put a meat grinder on mine

THE MAN IMPORTED FROM MEMPHIS:

One thing the white folks are going to have to learn—

white folks don't pick the leaders

for the black folks no more

MAYOR OF A TOWN ON THE MARCH ROUTE:

We are determined that they shall not ravish our homes

Our men are armed and determined

We are preparing to defend our civil institutions

the threat is coming from the east

He is a known criminal, said the mayor

probably a boaster, a braggart

We must assume that those who follow him

are of the same get

After that I would have followed Sweet Willie Wine into hell

THE MAN IMPORTED FROM MEMPHIS had never laid eyes on her before [this is not exactly a love story]:

She pulled up beside him on the curb, on the wrong side of the street.

He's dead! she yelled. He's dead!

Who's dead?

Hunter Crumb! He's dead!

[Having just seen the prosecutor in his office, having been there within the hour trying to obtain permits for the march, the Invader is taken aback.]

He says to himself, This crazy white woman thinks I killed him. Now she is going to kill me.

Come here, I want to give you something.

No, I don't think I'll be coming over there, ma'am.

No, come over here. I want to give you something.

[Mr. Invader thinks he's about to become Mr. Goner and politely declines to approach.]

She flings a gold chain at him and squalls off the curb. BLINGBLING.

That's how they met.

✝ ✝ ✝

IN LOUISVILLE, after the family farm was lost:

Her house, the house of her father and her stepmother, it was cold cold cold.

V'S FRIEND BIRDIE:

I always thought I would go to the university. Be a cheerleader.

Marry the captain of the football team. Have 2½ children.

And live on a cloud.

[Those were the days when people thought cars could fly

and the Russians sent their old to be melted down for candles.]

And V, well, she wanted something else.

No Russian ever called her [N-word lover].

Vines support an abandoned shack

Vines conceal abandoned farm implements

People are walking out of the ragged fields

Vines threaten the utility pole

Vines protect the copperhead from the hoe

Cottonwoods flutter as one

Bats at the cell tower

The tub in which James Earl Ray stood

to slay the King has sold online

[watch out for that phantom punch]

It's like a river running backwards

The Man Imported from Memphis

credits a rubber shrunken head

he wears around his neck

for keeping the skies overcast

and temperatures down

If white people can ride down the highways

with guns in their trucks

I can walk down the highway unarmed

Scott Bond, born a slave, became

a millionaire. Wouldn't you like to run wild

run free. The Very Reverend Al Green

hailed from here. Sonny Liston a few miles west,

Sand Slough. Head hardened

on hickory sticks. A reporter asks a family

of sharecroppers quietly watching the procession,

Does this walk means anything to you.

The father says, the others nod,

It means that Sweet Willie Wine is walking.

The cool water is for white/ the sun-heated for black

This chair is not for you [N-word]/ it is for the white buttock

This textbook/ is nearly new/ is not for you [N-word]

This plot of ground does not hold black bones

Today the sermon once again "Segregation After Death"

✝ ✝ ✝

After the pool was drained for the season, they arrested the kids who marched to the white school. Who stood and sang "Like a Tree Planted by the Water." They took them to the jailhouse in school buses. They took them to the drained pool in sealed 18-wheelers. The sheriff told them they were to be taken to the woods and there shot. Then the sheriff told them they were to be taken to the pool and there drowned.

GRANDDAUGHTER OF V'S BABYSITTER who was put in the pool she had never seen before then: He was one mean man. That sheriff.

A pool, a dry, drained pool, whatever else it is, is a big hole in the ground.

A sealed truck, whatever else it is, is a sealed truck.

THE SUPERINTENDENT: You people are heading for serious trouble if you don't stop this nonsense and leave these [whites only] grounds right this moment. You students are hereby expelled from this school district and if you don't get off the [sacred white] school grounds immediately, I'm going to have you arrested.

Headline: THE NEGROES FAIL TO MOVE

The weather could break.

The sheriff's button says Never.

The children's minds say Never waver.

V, rising to contempt: And that sheriff,

may he be taken to the woods and there

made to sing Like a Tree

Planted by the Water. May he

be linked to the first rib

he broke, and it be fashioned of

bronze. And run through the end

of his nose. He may then be

taken to the pool and there taught

the dead man's float. And then be

taken to the library and there will

his hideous pink testicles be removed

by the assistant librarian and put

in the terrarium with

the resident spider.

The ethical this, what we really want, says my friend Harry, is to get the present in the present, *that which is not this:* to feel and transmit.

The felony logs for that period are mostly devoted to burglary and grand larceny, bad checks, attempted escapes, embezzlement; possession of a machine gun for aggressive purposes [correction, possession of three machines guns]. A man killed his wife with a hammer. A man found in possession of a fifty-gallon mash barrel and cooker. And one poor fellow was popped for having unnatural relations with a cow.

The biggest hit is Al Green. And the biggest hitter is Sonny Liston.
The Silver Fox kind of stalled.

A Quaker protesting the war in Vietnam has set himself on fire in front of the Pentagon. He dropped the baby out of harm's way before he flicked open his lighter.

Phoenix is burning.

In August, Los Angeles burns for days, then Chicago.

Neck bones, 5 lb. a dollar.

The state's 1929 antievolution law is thought to be impossible to repeal.

V'S HUSBAND runs a notice in the paper: I will not be responsible for any

debts other than my own.

When she joined the marchers the husband's business went directly to

hell. When she was arrested. When they burned her car in the parking lot of the

station house. While she was in jail her husband bought airtime and denounced

her. When she was released she was served with papers for divorce and custody.

People were pointing the bone

at V. Women were supposed

to stay home. People were starving

the husband out. Men were supposed

to be in control. God's plan

for Big Tree. They tore a page straight

from the book. When he worked

for Philco they sent him

to the Halley Bay. He was shooting

little rockets into the aurora

borealis. That was the last good time,

the International Geophysical Year.

The earth, a greenish blue ball

streaked with clouds, spun on. The sky

filled with streamers of colored light.

I never knew what misery was till I came to Arkansas

✛ ✛ ✛

Or: what if all you wanted was to walk across that field at the fifty-yard line

on the arm of a boy wearing his shoulder pads lightly, as would you your faux

stole. [O high school, steer clear. You still suck.]

+ + +

Recruiting Office/ Right Turn Here

[I hope no one falls for that one.]

New Homes/ $0 Down

[I hope no one falls for that one.]

If your legs are trembling

try getting on your knees

[And they all fell down.]

DEAR ABBY,

Friends of ours have a son who has gone the hippies route. When we

inquire about their children [they have others who are married and one who is in

the service] should we ask about their hippie son? Or should we just not mention

him like he is "dead"? We know that they are pretty sick about the life he leads.

DEAR NEEDS TO KNOW,

Knowing that your friends would be humiliated or embarrassed by the mention of their hippie son, don't mention him.

Everybody has a problem. What's yours.

The movie was *Run Wild, Run Free.*

Come again.

✝ ✝ ✝

Her daddy, it was V's one and only boast, naturalized Thomas Merton.

Mother dead by the time she was three.

Father married her mother's sister.

Life on the farm was lonely with the mute and alcoholic father, the unloving, unlovable stepmother. Her only friend, a black hand named Wordan.

HER FIRST MEMORY is of a racial incident: I am sitting in a tub in an old kitchen. Wordan is washing my back. [N-word] you got soap in my eye, I must have said. Miss Olga, Missy done called me [N-word], Wordan must have said. I hear a German voice, my grandmother's, Wash her mouth out with soap. And he did, and to this day I hate Ivory Soap. It enrages me. She was close to four, dating by the new 1936 Chrysler her father brought home moments after her mouth was soaped. She does not know where she learned the slur but it would not burst from her again.

There are no memories of her mother. She was thirty-three. V was three. Wordan was taking her mother to the doctor and to buy a new cap for himself. She asked Wordan to drive her home. And he knew she was going to die because she forgot the cap. Coldest day of the year. She wanted the window open.

In Louisville, after the family farm was lost, her house, the house of her father and stepmother's, was cold cold cold.

HER CHILDHOOD FRIEND AND COUSIN: V always had good-looking legs and loved to sit in the sun.

Never allowed to do anything. About only thing she could do was read. Spent the night with her a couple of times. We put on gloves and wrote a letter to the principal.

Always for the underdog, whether it was a ballgame or a race war.

Always stealing a smoke behind the barn.

Always at the library. Always commingling with books she shouldn't have. She wrote a report on Le Père Goriot, which was on the librorum prohibitorum list [in effect until 1966].

Ask her to go anywhere. Answer always no. No, I can't, I have to listen to Bellini. No, I can't, I have to memorize Browning.

Read from caint to caint.

Oscar Wilde perverted me, she told me as a calcified fact.

The Brontës, Austen, Galsworthy, Cellini's *Autobiography* [I love it,
remarked V with relish, when he is forgiven for all murders past and to come].
Cyril Cusack came to her school to lecture on Hopkins. *Macbeth* came one year
as did an all-girl production of *Julius Caesar.*

I was totally smitten, she told me, with Mark Antony.

Memorized Cardinal Wolsey's speech. And recalls being shepherded
into the auditorium to watch General MacArthur on a little snowy television
mounted onstage.

Wordan kept an alligator. Built a cement pool for it in back. Drain and
everything.

V kept a retired fighting cock.

Helmet was her only pleasure.

That wasn't her favorite bird though. Her favorite bird was a shrike.

Now, you might be praying

for a fence or the ability to read

and write; you might be praying

for a better shift, a 50¢ raise;

you might be praying for a truck

that starts right up, a pair of long legs

or the recovery of a loving mother;

you might be praying for the safety

of your twins riding the bus

with a cold sack lunch

You have to watch hear me

how you carry yourself

Festina lente my darlings

King called it a disease, segregation. [Sounds contagious.]

Then there's the consolation of religion; whereas the promise cannot be broken if it applies only to the hereafter and thereafter; whereas herein things can remain in whatever order the ones with the most money and the most ammo say shall they stand.

RADIO MINISTRY: Now the nonrepentant homosexuals, they're declaring war on the Gospel. Now the infidels are dying from the neck up. Now I didn't write the Bible. Now your old-line churches are losing members. Now if I'm going to be saved, I have to be saved from something, the vile and the dirty and your low-downs. It's not like joining the Rotary Club. Salvation, it's a heaven or hell issue.

Now V, she wanted something

entirely different:

To feel and transmit/ The ethical this

that is not that

The Gospel helps some bear the pain/ helps

bury the hate

The swimming pool is also buried therein

and therefore this

Petition for relief/ Awaken to the task

Call for calm/ Waver never

Forever forward/ Backwards never

it says on the ex-Invader's machine

The dirt up there

on the Ridge is called loess

Windblown stuff

good for growing peaches

Hemingway penned

some of *A Farewell to Arms*

on the Ridge when he was married

to Pauline [wife number two]

The marchers make fifteen miles a day in spite of the heat

I think my arches have fallen

says the Invader to the stringer

Oh yeah, I remember her, she celebrated all her kids'

birthdays on the same day

I met the retired welding teacher at the Colonel's. We were the only

customers. He had a big soft drink. We sat in the lipstick red booth. He was a

veteran. He thought he would never come back to Big Tree, but he did:

This was his sky, his clouds rucked up over the fields. The blackbirds flashing

their red shoulders. His country. He gave all the credit to God and His plan.

He was drafted and got arrested right before he went to boot camp, stops to

add: That wasn't the first thing we did though.

Before he left for Nam, there was something he had to do.

He and Toad and some other buddies, they were going to that bowling alley. They were going bowling. Toad had a truck, and come Sunday, come Sunday evening they were going.

There were four of us. And when we came over the rise to where you see the bowling alley on your left, there were more white people than I ever saw in my life.

Someone knew, someone told.

The bowling alley is long gone. Burned. I cruise over the rise in my rental car. There is an electrical and plumbing supply place. A collection of prefab structures.

It could not look more ahistorical.

I think of him coming over the rise, ten thousand times since then, and every single time, sensing a turbulence in the air above the surface of his skin. The way when my daddy took us back to his homestead, and we would pass a certain farmhouse, he would say, There was a murder in that house when I was a boy. It caused a great commotion.

Some thing happened on that spot. No one was shot. No one got strung up, but belligerent men glommed in a parking lot.

Some one among them said, We aren't going to do anything to you. Whoever it was that spoke was heeded, a narrow channel formed through which the young African American men could go forward to the glass door. They are cursed, spat upon, mocked, threatened. Then they hear a tremendous crash. The truck, Toad's truck has been hove on its side. But the one of their number in front, maybe James, opens the door, walks inside, picks up a ball [it had to be a ladies' ball, blue and speckled like a mockingbird's egg] and lets it drop down a lane or down the gutter [he does not linger to see if a pin falls]; turns and walks out. The four move as one to the overturned truck and hoist it upright, climb aboard, not a word spoken. Toad pops the clutch.

After that, was the bowling alley integrated.

After that, it burned.

After that, we tried to integrate the lunch counter at Harmon's.

What happened.

They tore out the lunch counter.

The marchers are resting in the city park. They dine on neck bones, black-eyed peas, and soft drinks.

No incidents have been reported.

Well, what about so-and-so, I say. He's not a bad sort.

Yes, but a well-meaning white man, he can just go so far. So we beat him at the polls. It was time. It did not mean we would get a better man for the job, but we would get shed of the skin of the injuring parties. It is something that had to be done.

I ask if he has any memory of any good-intentioned whites.

Had a little old cleaning job. An older man came in while I was sweeping. He called me [N-word]. Bawled me out for stirring up dust. The owner came from out behind the counter, moving fast-like and close-up. Don't you ever call him out of his name again, you hear me. That was a stand-up moment he would not forget. He could not recall any other.

IN HELL'S KITCHEN, she is dying in her chair. We watch an old black-and-white on television; we see the man's black arm. We see his serving arm. He carries a tray and his arm enters the screen, some tender band of wrist is exposed. With glasses balanced just so, and a white napkin draped over his forearm. He has no speaking part. And the rest of him stays out of sight. An invisible man.

Any simple problem can be made insoluble.

God's plan. We go on thanking Him for all these benisons which are theirs. This is not His fault. Baby Jesus is not to blame. He is just a blameless little old baby. So like our own.

El sueño de la razón produce monstruos. The print on her wall, torn from a tired-out book. Goya, she would have run off with, if he'd only asked.

✝ ✝ ✝

FORMER STATE LEGISLATOR: I edged out the representative who introduced legislation to label the blood. White blood/black blood.

After a recount.

Got beat by the sheriff who told the kids they were to be taken to the woods and there shot.

Got beat by the sheriff who told the kids they were to be taken to the pool and there drowned.

Beat by the sheriff who told the farmers that posted the blanket bond he would call the claim on their deeds if they voted against him and then would he take their lands.

Beat by the sheriff who kept a man's testicles in a jar on his desk until the word got around; he flushed them to the underworld from which no smoke escapes.

Bought a color TV from her husband the year the Longhorns beat the Hogs.

By one measly point in the last fifteen minutes. Game of the Century it was

touted.

The Big Shootout. In the stands were Lyndon Baines Johnson, George

Herbert Walker Bush, and the reigning Richard Milhous Nixon, and one row

back, a pair of trademark black-rims. The Very Reverend Billy Graham prayed

over all. The field was all-white.

William Jefferson Clinton listened on shortwave from Oxford.

But the band didn't play "Dixie."

Come again.

Only that the band didn't play "Dixie."

Just a few days into the draft lottery. A few days after the Peace with

Justice Resolution. [Peace with Justice for whom do you think.]

Clinton drew #311. [But he was already 1-A.]

Same day the Big Bear set off a nuclear test and the Stones played at
Altamont. [It was the end of something was it not.]

✝ ✝ ✝

HER FRIEND BIRDIE: She was never a whiner or complainer. She might
rage for a minute in the most colorful language and then that was that. Back to
the more interesting conversation she preferred.

Did she have a priest at the end.

I had to tell her that I thought a priest would enter at his own peril.

Hahahahahaha, Birdie wrote back.

BIRDIE: I did not see her again after she crossed over.

This was when the hotdog wagon doubled as a whorehouse on wheels.
[Picture that if you can.]

Temperatures are in the 90s even after a shower.

The threat is coming.

This belonged to her mother. Though she had no memory

of the woman and she may have never worn it. And this,

her father's. In his vest

when he fell, draft of a poem in the hand

of one Thomas Merton to one grey-eyed nurse, M,

his midsummer secret.

These were the pictures on one shelf in the Hell's Kitchen apartment [from

books or newspapers or postcards]. In one frame, from left to right: Wilde, Yeats,

Eliot, Joyce, Blake, Rimbaud, Baudelaire, Shakespeare, Proust—her gang of guy scribes.

On the same shelf: a clipping of the four girls murdered in the 16th Street Baptist Church bombing; pictures of Malcolm X, Trotsky, Castro in 1959; a Palestinian killed in Gaza, an AP image from the Louisville *Courier* of the last day of the Vietnam War [a picture I borrowed from V to use on the cover of the first edition of *The Battlefield Where the Moon Says I Love You* by the poet Frank Stanford].

Two family photos, one of her father, a prominent [besotted] lawyer who headed up the regional immigration bureau. And one of Wordan who worked on the family farm and moved with them to Louisville. He left once and moved to East St. Louis. His wife was murdered there. He was alone again. Wordan came back.

It was a lonely childhood to say the least. Mother dead. Stepmother removed. Father more remote. Grandmother severe. And Wordan, sole companion to the little blond girl. He was not Mr. Bojangles. She was not Shirley Temple.

RETIRED WELDING TEACHER at the Colonel's: My brother had

an injustice done to him. He was wrongfully accused. Wrongfully charged.

Wrongfully prosecuted. Convicted. My brother was innocent. And that wasn't

the worst. They knew. They knew it all along. But he was out there. He had a

little old job delivering groceries. He was on his bicycle. Sacks in the basket

when they picked him up.

This boy and this girl were caught kissing. Caught by an uncle who

screamed rape. And the first young man the police saw on their side of

town—my brother, pedaling his bicycle, they picked him up. They picked him up.

Kicked. Clubbed. Cuffed. Charged. Convicted him. Just like that. The girl never

took the stand. She was never in the courtroom. Her uncle. We don't know what

he did to her. We just know what he caused done to my brother.

THE BROTHER TO WHOM A CERTAIN INJUSTICE WAS DONE [who

lives in Reno]: One night after the conviction, the police let me go in the middle

of the night. Just like that. I showed up on Mother's porch. The police told me to

get out of town before dawn. So the family pitched in and bought me a one-way

ticket to San Francisco and I went. Believe you me, I went.

How did you feel when you first saw those golden gates.

You got me there.

People wore purple pants.

Come again.

In California, people wore purple pants.

And he did not come back and he did not come back and he did not come

back. Clickety clack.

And V, lived in a box with a man who fixed clocks fixed clocks fixed clocks.

✛ ✛ ✛

HER OLDEST DAUGHTER, MAY, was playing at the spring across town

when the word went out about the shooting at the Lorraine Motel. I best go

home she told her playmate. Her mother was pacing up and down on the porch,

blowing smoke. They did it she said. They killed him. The King is gone.

THE MAN IMPORTED FROM MEMPHIS, the Invader: I had only been out of prison a short time. I was making my rounds. I stopped to see some friends on Hernando Street. Stopped in L'il Ella's. They asked what should they do if King got killed, and I said, Nothing to do but go on home.

Later, I was out walking and a woman yelled at me, Go get 'em, son. Go get 'em. I didn't know what she was talking about. Stopped back in at L'il Ella's and they heard it on the radio. I said, Go home, just go on home now. And the women got up with soap in their hair and left out of the shop. Next day I was sitting in the chair at home—something told me to go; my body lifted itself from the chair. I walked to Vance. I could see a silent crowd; my body carried me to Lewis & Sons where the King was laid out. Afterwards I went to the Invaders and said I was ready.

To act, just to act. That was the glorious thing.

Since I have been with the Movement, I have not committed any so-called crime. The Movement is the best thing I've ever been involved in.

OLDEST DAUGHTER, MAY, wanted to know: Did she tell me about her
mother getting a Jheri curl.

[I have no clue what that is.]

When she crossed over, she still had to get her hair done. That was not a
luxury, it was a necessity. She could not go to her old hairdresser. If she did,
he would lose his shop; so she crossed over Division. Got a Jheri curl. It was a
disaster. After that she wore it cropped short. She wore a Little Dutch Boy cut
when beehives were big.

HER FRIEND BIRDIE: Did not see V again after she crossed over. Ever.
Though she loved her. But she did not, and she could not.

Headline: WHITE WOMAN BACKS NEGROES, LOSES FRIENDS

It would be true to say, Birdie believed in V. It would be true to say, she
loved her friend. And would miss her for the rest of her days.

BIRDIE: Could not confirm the long-standing rumor about the hotdog
wagon.

Wildlife Federation has called off its annual picnic.

Temperatures reached mid-90s early in the day. Following a shower.

IN THE HELL'S KITCHEN APT: There were shelves crammed with votive candles and tchotchkes—most prized, a Niki de Saint Phalle powder jar with a golden serpent coiled up on its lid. Inside was a clipping of the artist's obituary. V's pewter crèche, her Balinese puppets.

IN HELL'S KITCHEN: She had the Harvard Classics, but she had the hots for the new stuff, same as she did the old. The Classics came from her father. Missing one volume of the English poets, though she read Swinburne at school. [She claimed the Sacred Heart library wasn't half bad.] She also claimed to despise Browning who was her father's favorite. On the subject of books that was her only stated instance of rebellion because she was as taken with them as was her silent, pickled old man. At the time of her death, she had made significant headway into collecting folio editions of every title she had eaten as a child.

Once, she mentioned that she was able to name the baby she gave up for adoption: Stephen.

THIS IS ONE OF THE THINGS I HEAR HAPPENED: She has just folded herself over to brush off the brown leaves covering her coleus. She has been stacking wood. She has on the work glove. She is going back inside to clean up; she bends from the waist to make a quick pass at the leaves that she might still enjoy the tart color of on her coleus a bit longer. She feels a quick sting, thinks it's a wasp or a hornet and goes inside [the light at the sink is better]. As soon as the glove is off and she grabs the baking soda to put on the spot, she notes the rapid swelling in the webbing between her thumb and index [her hands her best feature, better than the legs even], the throb, already throbbing, and steps back outside to check if it was a hornet or wasp and glimpses as she peers into the coleus the dusty reddish thing, the sickening hourglasses along its thick length as it creeps soundlessly into the foliage, and it passes through her mind as her body is passing out that Southerners sympathizing with the North were called Copperheads.

AND, vacuuming the rag rug, listening to Nina Simone: The record had a catch in it. Always started over at "Old Jim Crow is dead." When the phone rang, and she shut off the vacuum cleaner, not the record player, and the caller said Hunter [expletive] Crumb is dead.

VINDICATION

After that she would have followed Sweet Willie Wine into hell.

Her husband would come home from work and she would be in a rage, and he could not understand it. He would repair to his shed to build his models.

There is a sanctuary in the mind made of balsa and glue. Perfect little gliders constructed in perfect quietude.

There is a sanctuary in the mind made of poetry and music and laughter. Whiskey and cigarettes never run out, and the ironing board is never in use.

There is a sanctuary without the stench of diapers, the drone of the sewing machine, or the fretful pawing of rosaries.

DEAR ABBY,

My mother-in-law said she read in your column about how to make dirty diapers disappear.

DEAR MISINFORMED,

I am not a magician.

Everybody has a problem.

Once and once only, she mentioned: He may have been conceived in the middle of the Ohio River, Stephen.

THE MAN IMPORTED FROM MEMPHIS, the Invader: I don't see many of the Invaders anymore. Coby is still here. Cabbage is here. Drives a cab. J Smith went back to Atlanta and got a Ph.D. Calvin works for the convention center. Marrell, works for the CIA. Before that, undercover for the Memphis police. [Seconds after the assassination, he was on the balcony.] Don, he was an informant too, we became good friends. Gwin, the one that was cut in the attack, she went to Nebraska. King Jewel faded from the scene. I don't know what happened to Cornbread. Can't remember his last name. Saw his sister not too long ago.

Eddie T was wild. Couldn't do a thing with him. Heard he died in Cummins Prison. His wife stayed in Big Tree a long time. I had never heard of Big Tree before I got the call. I had never crossed that bridge to Arkansas.

I went to prison twice. Last time I stirred things up—about conditions—the crowding, the food, and so on. They put me in what had been the women's unit. Little old knee-high fence. Fished all the time. When I got out, I went back to seeing everybody on Beale and Hernando. Things were going on in Memphis.

Now I wonder whatever happened to Cornbread.

V, deep down, she may have been as sad as a cover band. She might have felt drier than a clod of Arkansas dirt. Lonely lonely lonely, like the hunter green suitcase that hadn't been used since her honeymoon.

Some honeymoon, she later told Gert, with that off-color smile, she almost had to rape him. She said this near death. As her executive organs were shutting down and she was finishing the *NYT* crossword, September 2, in ballpoint:

What is a suffix of book

ish

Who is a major exporter of coconut oil

Samoa

A colorless liquid

ouzo

A defeatist's words

I [nospace] lose

The artist of the etching and aquatint, *el sueño de la razón produce monstruos.*

[*Does it follow that the sleep of monsters produces reason?*]

It was the Thursday *Times*. They get harder. But the others got thrown out. This was on a shelf of dust under the silhouette where a boomerang had hung. The boomerang's silhouette and the telephone's and the outline of her iconoclastic altar, stayed white. Otherwise the walls were solid nicotine.

Had cancer after she had her last baby. Had a hysterectomy. Didn't want anyone to know because she thought they'd say, *That poor woman with all those children and now she's got cancer.* An invisible woman.

In Hell's Kitchen, in her shaky hand, in soft pencil, next to the sill overlooking the scraggly barren pear in front of her building she wrote:

Cheops 2575 BC–2150 BC

Moses 13th c. BC–Homer 9th c. BC

Hesiod 8th c. BC–Herodotus 485–425 BC

Socrates 469–399 BC

V, if I may ask why did you write that on your wall.

It's handy. It settles a lot of arguments, and with growing enthusiasm,

That's not the first thing I wrote on the wall though, the first thing I wrote is over here:

Unless a proposition is necessary it is meaningless with meaning approaching zero. —Burroughs

I still haven't figured it out, she adds with obvious pleasure. Then I wrote:

Be still, the hanging gardens were a dream. —Trumbull Stickney

After she died the photographer and I visit the apartment. I find what she scribbled next to where her phone had hung:

WHAT

FRESH

HELL

IS

THIS

below which:

INTERPOSITION

AND

NULLIFICATION

And a sampling from her own hagiography, the names:

Elegua [the trickster, guardian of the crossroads, messenger to god, lover of children; his numbers are 3 and 21; his day is Monday and his colors are black and red; his offerings are candy, cigars, and rum, and those too you would find on her shelves]

Saint Anthony [to help her find things buried in the archaeology of her apartment]

Santa Barbara [to protect her from lightning]

Obatala [king of the white cloth—a benign deity by the measure and history of the world's big-brand religions, minus some sacrificial chickens and an occasional goat—the essence of purity, justice, and clear thinking, but overly fond of palm wine; one with whom she might have identified]

Ben Turpin [the cross-eyed silent film comedian]

✝✝✝

When I check into THE PEABODY the Jingle Bell Ball is about to begin. The lobby is jammed with tweens in designer dresses.

Lansky Brothers has moved its store into the Peabody from its old storefront on Beale Street. Tailor to Elvis, the Man in Black, and the johns of Beale.

And there he is Mr. Lansky, walking the floor, incarnate, draped in his measuring tape. Proverbial spring in his step. Inept at retiring, even at aging.

Mr. Lansky, did you know Henry Loeb, the late and former mayor.

I knew Henry very well. Big ox of a man, 6'4". He wore those white bucks, says the tailor to Elvis, the tailor to Johnny Cash, the tailor to the mayor of Memphis on whose watch the country lost its King.

Some leaders grow small and some grow tall in perpetuity.

Moved to Big Tree after all that went on.

Old King Cotton. He was never the real king. There was only the one King.

GRADUATE FROM ALL-WHITE HIGH SCHOOL, First Year of Choice:
When MLK died kids were laughing and talking about how they should have
killed that [N-word] a long time ago.

Did you hear the one about the [N-word] that...

Do you know why the colored want to send their children to the white
school.
So they can learn to read and riot.

Do you know what they sang at King's funeral.
Bye-bye, blackbird.

Memphis has one up on Dallas.
They got a president. We got a king.

So they slew the dreamer, and ever since they've been trying to slay the dream.

GRADUATE OF ALL-WHITE HIGH SCHOOL, First Year of Choice: Tried to
time my trips to the restroom. Pick the right time I'd be alone with the sink and

the mirror. Pick wrong, the smoking girls leaned against the sink in front of the mirror, Something stinks in here, smells like a [N-word].

Henry did not seek reelection. A fourth-generation Memphian. Wealthy. Jewish. Episcopalian. Big ox of a man. Liked to wear white bucks. Moved to Big Tree of all places. Big spread up on the Ridge. Sold farm implements. Had plenty of money. Made more money. Moved to be among those of his own get.

It's almost closing time at the CIVIL RIGHTS MUSEUM, Lorraine Motel. I walk down to Mulberry, past big vacant blocks. I move quickly past the displays of dry-mounted text and props from the Movement and wend my way to room 306.

Looking through the Plexiglas that separates us from the carefully unkempt furnishing at the Lorraine—cigarette butts in the ashtray and the dinner plate shared with Abernathy.

The stuck clock of history.

An anachronistic-looking child stands next to me, with ringlets like Shirley Temple. Is this where they killed Elvis she asked her mother.

Wrong king child, wrong freaking king.

CRUISING DOWN UNION AVE: Why there's Nathan Bedford Forrest, confident as ever on the one mount out of nearly thirty that didn't get shot out from under him.

Those hoofbeats die not

TAPED TO A UTILITY BOX, corner of Highland and Poplar:

I'm tired of hearing what rich people have to say

STOPOVER AT BURKE'S BOOKS:

Graffiti in the bathroom:

What the American public does not know

is what makes the American public. —Anonymous

I slept with Bill Faulkner. —Anonymous

Along the wall lined with the author photos, I pick out Joan Williams. [*She slept with Bill.*]

✝ ✝ ✝

FAMILY OF V'S BABYSITTER: Another stifling day in Big Tree. There was a fight on the South Side, a family disturbance that got loud, got ugly. Cops came. There were arrests. Her father went to the jailhouse to find out about his sons. They wouldn't tell him anything. They wouldn't let him post bail. He got a call late that night. The sons were going to be released. He went down there. In the a.m. hours they let them go. First they cut the outside lights. A line of pickups were idling in the lot. The men in the trucks, the patriarch knew them all. They were from the farms. He was the flat-fixer for every one of those farms. They said they were going to take them to a fish fry. It was a [N-word] fry. That's what it was. They beat her father. Beat the crap out of him. The youngest boys ran off. One jumped from the overpass. His knees jammed. Permanently. The brothers scrambled under a vehicle in a carport. The patriarch hid in the sticker bushes. He couldn't see. He bled until he blacked out.

Maybe the reverend knew they were under his vehicle. Maybe he didn't.

He held his tongue. It was a choreographed release. Don't you see. The police

notified the men on the farms, the Night Riders, gave them time to get together.

The flat-fixer knew every one of them. And they knew him.

✝ ✝ ✝

VIETNAM VETERAN, RETIRED NURSE: We were in the second wave

of arrests. We met at the funeral home and broke into groups of fourteen. That

way we were legal. A lot of us still got arrested and transported in horse trailers

to the dressing room of the pool. Took three of us in the dogcatcher wagon.

I was eighteen. Graduated and went to Vietnam. Wounded. Purple Heart.

Came home and town under curfew.

I picked my mother up from church. My car was surrounded. A woman held

a brick. She saw I had a Service .45. I said, Lady, you hit my car...

Hardest part to come back and see signs that said [N-word].

All my kids were military. Oldest son killed by police officer in Memphis. Had a great job, went to church, great family. Now the cop is dead. He was black too.

Jesus saved me from the hatred. It's the only way.

When life gets you down/ keep looking up

✛ ✛ ✛

RETIRED WELDING TEACHER: Kept first watch on the porch with the lights off. Wore my fatigues. Holding a rifle. Since Nam, we were armed, too.

That's when things began to calm down. When both sides were armed. Black people coming back from the Mekong Delta toting M16s, the way we used to walk off the fields with hoes.

There was a shooting at the Tastee-Freez. Things got too dangerous and kind of chilled off.

A teacher has been fired for a derogatory letter, for insubordination in which he told the superintendent the Negro had no voice.

It was a riot, a rampage. An outbreak. A disturbance. The students called it a boycott, a walkout. Gentle Reader, it was an uprising.

During the morning of this date, no one had been given any cause to believe that a riot was imminent. However the superintendent had notified the chief of the firing of a teacher at the all-Negro junior high and had stated that there might be trouble.

The first teacher to approach the study hall after the disturbance began was not on hall duty but went on the basis of a report that there was trouble.

When he arrived there was not another teacher in the study hall. The students were then in the process of overturning tables and throwing chairs.

The students, by this time numbering in the hundreds, went out upon the grounds; some or all of them continued their course of conduct throwing bottles, rocks, or other objects at the building resulting in breakage of glass.

A bottle or some other object struck an assistant superintendent on the forehead inflicting a moderately severe wound requiring medical attention.

WE [the grand jury] are aware that every effort is being made to bring about better facilities, yet we feel that this alone will not cure the ills that exist. Whether it be crowded conditions, lack of discipline, lack of respect, political and/or social ills, or imagined political or social ills, none of these excuse or justify damage and destruction of our education institutions.

> Immediate Steps
>
> Must Be Taken
>
> Toward More Strict
>
> Position Of Discipline,
>
> Respect, Order
>
> Quickly As Possible
>
> Closer Observation
>
> Take Whatever Steps
>
> Necessary
>
> Bring It
>
> Immediately

Under Control

Protect Property

Rights Of Those

Desiring

Deserving

Opportunity

Education

Our County Judge

Doing Excellent Job

[later sent up for racketeering]

Under Circumstances

Best Crime Deterrent

Sure Detection

Swift Apprehension

Certain Punishment

Testimony Shows

An Excess Of $19,000

Spent Restoring

The Building

To Habitable Condition

A month later it was unofficially reported that a walkout was in progress at the all-Negro senior high.

Langston's word was *fester.*

King's was *thingification.* The *thingification of our humanity.*

What the King called *nobodiness.*

Festina lente, with all deliberate speed, make haste slowly. Voluntary gradualism, glacial time.

THE D.A. said it was not in the public interest to bargain with any evildoers; they had no cause to meet with or make concessions to any bush-league agitators from Little Rock, nor for that matter, with any hoodlum parasite element.

He speaks he claimed for the judge, the sheriff, the city, and himself.

THE CHIEF [former bouncer at the Cotton Club]: They got to yeah-yeahing each other. The whites have taken it off of them until they've got tired of it.

THE CONCERNED CITIZENS COUNCIL's first guest speaker [over cookies and punch at their new offices in the former city barbershop]: The rule of the majority is being eroded by the minority.

MAYOR: I don't think they have any real grievance.

COUNTY JUDGE: I assure you we've been nothing but good to the [N-word].
Come again.

You've got me, man, said the Invader to his assailants.
You've got me. [It was not part of his plan to die in Arkansas.]

THE PUBLISHER says this community has no quarrel with its Negro citizens, to the contrary, the average white and Negro citizen in Big Tree get along as well as citizens in any city anywhere in the world; the problem lies in the hands of a small minority of troublemakers who seem hell-bent on making

Big Tree a focal point of racial unrest. The time for pacifying them is past. Our officials have no alternative now but to meet them head-on.

HEAD OF THE BIRCHERS [that backdoor abortionist] told newsmen [over cookies and punch] that the president was leading the nation toward insolvency, surrender, and socialism.

DEAR ABBY,

My daughter married a 30-year-old mama's boy who is in love with tropical fish. He has 13 tanks of them. Just to give you an idea he paid $14 for 1 little fish.

DEAR MOTHER,

Water seeks its own level—even in a fish tank.

What's your problem.

Lions cancel annual picnic due to concerns.

Spinster luncheon honors fiancée [an attractive blonde]

of Mr. Peacock.

County board recommends dismissal of Negro caseworker.

Death of a Gunfighter ends Wednesday.

ELSEWHERE:

Camille pummels Gulf.

Israeli jets attack Egypt.

Squads ready to break up Irish riots.

Sept 3 marks the death of Ho.

✝ ✝ ✝

Harry says, What we really want from our time on this planet, is *that which is not this,* we want *the ethical this;* we want to feel and transmit.

It is known that when a blackbird calls in the marsh all sound back and if one note is missing all take notice. This is the solidarity we are born to.

King said no one could be an outsider who lived inside these borders. There are no Invaders.

What the white man wanted, no less than complete control.

Who expected the sidewalks cleared when they came down them [as in the days of the Raj].

✝ ✝ ✝

The boys hid under the reverend's vehicle. I can't say if the reverend knew they were there. I can't say if he didn't know. He probably knew. They hid on the concrete slab under the block. They held their breath and listened. One of them was hurt pretty bad. And the patriarch, the flat-fixer, lost an eye.

Hateful words survive in sticky clumps

Furry thoughts skid across the yellow line

And over the muddy embankment.

Big enough to hunt, being hunted.

Says the sheriff, Nowadays you can't

Even say chigger you have to say Cheegro.

They fired the flat-fixer. They fired him after they put out his eye. The eel
in the L'Anguille never were. The flat-fixer who said he'd get the radio fixed. He
knew who could fix it. They fired him. Never held an eel, she just slithered. The
fixer, they said, stole their shortwave. He had it fixed. They fired him. But first
they put out his eye. So they named it L'Anguille. And the Mississippi receives
them both, but you wouldn't notice now. It's casino to casino from here to the
Big Easy. The other river, that would be the St. Francis.

They said they would take this harm. They would take it this time, would
move on. They would walk away, walk away. Turn a blind eye. They would

go forward into the seasons of their lives. They would see the sun shiver as

it disappeared behind willow and cottonwood, the blackbird threading the

phone lines, the combine continuing to rust on its haunches. They would not be

deformed by this hatefulness. Nor be comforted by religion [though would be

their women]. But if anyone ever touched any of them ever again. They would

put this town on the map. They made their pact. They took the no-quarter oath.

They were eight men strong. And they meant it, Gentle Reader. They meant it.

Outside of North Little Rock they are joined by a Quaker.

From ONE TOO YOUNG TO JOIN THE UPRISING: The all-Negro

elementary school was behind the all-Negro junior high. They were letting us

out early. The troopers were there. We wanted to see. We wanted to see the

goings-on. I got to watch a couple of chairs fly out the window is all. And here

come my loving mother to keep her baby out of harm's way.

THE RETIRED WELDING TEACHER: After they put us in the pool, they

taunted us. With chimp chants. They brought a TV and set it up and made us

watch Tarzan. They wouldn't let us sleep. They made us watch.

ONE OF THE STUDENTS ARRESTED AND PUT IN THE POOL: They arrested us in the morning and drove us around until dark. They told us all kind of things. But we didn't know what they were going to do with us. The last thing my mother said before I left the house—Don't you get in that line. Don't you get in that line, girl. Stay away. Remain calm. I won't even come see you if you go to jail. But later I found out she did try to see me. They gave us hand-me-down books. Turn to page 51, the teacher would say. It would be torn out. Lunch was slabs of butter between two pieces of bread. Milk usually spoiled and it cost 2¢.

GRADUATE OF ALL-WHITE HIGH SCHOOL, First Year of Choice: You have to understand about my mom, if she calls us up at three in the morning, and says, she wants ice cream, you get dressed and go buy ice cream. Even if you have to drive to Memphis. If she says talk to this woman, you talk.

Teachers' kids stuck together. We were the only ones with a telephone, a TV, a record player.

Blew the front of our house off the day before my father's funeral.

I see someone from that school now and think, I wonder if your father is still alive and if he is still wearing his little Klan outfit on Saturday night.

All of us who went to the white school have a story. Houlie went to Liberia. My husband never went back in the building.

HER MOTHER: I accept nothing less than respect. You hear me.

I haven't seen the lightning bugs yet but I do enjoy them. And by day I enjoy the butterflies. I sit on my step; they flutter around me. And I think, well maybe somebody is paying me a visit.

A teacher sent a note home saying she couldn't understand my oldest daughter. I told her I curse better than you speak. My daughter is not going to flunk English because you cannot speak it. No less than respect, you get what I'm saying.

The department store hired a couple of light-skinned blacks to work in the back [Saturdays only].

I remember her. Bought an Emerson from her husband for the Big
Shootout.

Parents came down with food for the kids when we found out where they
were. Police threw the burgers over the fence.

The former legislator said he fished with a man who told him the school
wouldn't be there when he came to teach in the fall, first year of Choice.

They march along here, the military road

The road they walk built by humpers

Those were the Irish

They pass Blackfish Lake

Ditch #1 about where they crossed

Gerstaecker slept here bundled up in a buffalo's skin

But first the Choctaw Removal; then came the Creek with ponies;

Then Chickasaw; then Cherokee, maybe Sequoyah among them his
syllabary nearly finished

Now stood another anonymous racist calling them names

His rod extended/ his line hung up in his own ignominy

THE MAN IMPORTED FROM MEMPHIS: When you get change you
keep pushing and you get more. The hardest thing is to get the ball rolling.

We are marching to get this fear out of your hearts. You must remember the white man puts his pants on the same way you do, one leg at a time.

Since I have been involved with the Movement I have not committed any so-called crime.

The Movement is the best thing I've ever been involved in. It channeled my energy into constructive efforts.

My aunt raised me. She worked as a domestic for the family of Judge Bailey Brown.

If white people can ride down their highways with guns, I can walk down the highway unarmed.

Old enough to hunt, hunted.

When people have anticipated something and they have been let down, you must find some way to let them use up this excess energy. [That, Gentle Reader, is the accursed share.]

My walk will help do this for the people of Arkansas. Not a question of violence or nonviolence. Survival is the point. We are going to survive one way or the other. Sweet Willie Wine, V, and the Invaders are

Walking we are just walking

Dead doe on the median

Whoever rides into the scene changes it

Pass a hickory dying on the inside

A black car that has not moved for years

Forever forward/ backwards never

+ + +

IN HELL'S KITCHEN: Her apartment is smaller by half than the shotgun shacks that used to stubble the fields outside of Big Tree. Stained from decades of nonstop smoking. The world according to V was full of smoke and void of mirrors.

She was not an eccentric. She was an original. She was congenitally incapable of conforming. She was resolutely resistant.

Her low-hanging fears no match for her contumacy

Grappling hooks in the mud leaf out in the mind

She was my goombah.

Cats, Catholicism, alcohol, and men. She served them all.

Children—she failed her own. Of that she was acutely aware. It was the grief of her existence.

If I could summon her L'wha now. If this were her book of days. If she were still able to sit back on her double-joints and read my cards: "Sometimes you feel rather alone in the world; times of stress and dissatisfaction are likewise times of passion..." If she were to pass through that wall this very second...

V, what spurred you to get involved.

It was when they put the kids in the swimming pool. My babysitter's granddaughter. They put her in the pool.

I knew some kids over at Memphis State and they put me in touch with the Invaders. I met one Invader and he wouldn't have anything to do with me. I wanted them to come over and help.

After I was driven out of Arkansas I went to the FBI office in Memphis. He said, What are you going to do. You know, you're not stupid. I said I don't know. He said why don't you take the civil service test. I took the civil service telephone operator's test and I was the top passer.

I got a letter back that said, With your infamous acts there is no way we would employ you. It was creepy. I wish I'd kept that letter. I could probably have sued them. I could have gone to Europe and lived awhile.

She was guilty of no fear, no envy, no meanness, and when if once-in-a-knocked-up-again moon she felt a twinge of desire for a certain silk blouse, she was sure to touch the wearer, to touch the other on the sleeve that she not be afflicted by any such shallow tendencies.

I remember her in livid color. Her with the *radiant cool eyes hallucinating Arkansas and Blake-light tragedy. The best mind*[ ] *of* [*a*] *generation* in an era, a place that thought nothing of a woman, even a white woman—and of a black woman, thought even less than.

The air itself was heavy upon them, the forward-marching folks who seemed small in number and dwindling in spirit. The King was dead; the laws were in place, but nobody said BOO about enforcement. [Well, yes, they did, they said INTERPOSITION AND NULLIFICATION.]

V: In high school, you are crazy for boys then. A cousin had a boy I sort of liked. He talked anti-Jewish. I told him I was half-Jewish. And that was that.

Concealed her pregnancy until she was seven months. I'm glad your mother is dead, her stepmother told her, her mother's sister.

I tried to get her first semester transcript, but there was none. She either did not finish the term or the records were lost or destroyed. I just wanted to see those easily won high marks. Who knows, they may have been punitively low. There was the book report from the pope's banned books list; the teacher who didn't know Swinburne; the biology teacher who said Jesus had 23 chromosomes and was the spit and image of his mother. Hahahahaha.

[That one busted her up.]

Walking they are just walking

Play the situation by ear

Inspiring fear/ Dispelling fear

Hateful words survive in sticky clumps

+ + +

MAYOR OF A TOWN ON THE MARCH ROUTE: With his twisted,
diseased mind you don't know what he's going to do.

THE GOVERNOR calls for the march to be ignored.

AN UNIDENTIFIED WOMAN carries a small red Bible.

Along the route, ARMED MEN IN FERTILIZER BINS.

MAYOR: It gives a man a place to stand so he won't be tempted to hurt them.

[They would kill us if they had the chance.]

V: We had the water and the shoes in my car. Stiles kept that water good and cold.

COUNCILMAN: We got good [N-word] here except for a few teens.

It is something you came through that.

It is the most alive I ever felt.

+ + +

HELL'S KITCHEN: I don't know what we're watching. She's in her puffy

chair, a few feet from her designated deathbed. When she sleeps it's in the

pleather chair, in front of her television. The bed has gathered dust and old hair

and the bugs that live on our slough. The leading man is dying. He is fitted in a

silk robe with tuxedo lapels. He lies in a big poster bed. He has but a handful of

breaths left in him.

She says to me, He doesn't want to leave his monogrammed pillowslip.

She says to me, I am Rafferty, the poet/ Eyes without sight

Mind without torment/ Going west on my journey

HER OLDEST DAUGHTER, MAY: Daddy caught a crow once. On the way

to school [apropos of nothing].

Wordan kept a pet alligator.

Mother kept a fighting cock [retired].

Called him Helmet.

BIRDIE: Did she have a priest.

He would have had to enter at his peril.

Hahahahaha.

+ + +

V is propped up and alert. A man lately helped with a little problem of a romantic nature has sent a white rose for every year of her life. Big old-fashioned smelling roses. She stays conscious until they drop their last petal. She stays with us for them.

We have come together in Hell's Kitchen, the old Memphis crowd. We stay up eating and drinking and talking more than either, and sleep in a heap; then some of us go to the demonstration. V is animated and tries to eat to humor us. We remind her of her kids crammed in their beds, telling the same old ghost story, the man with the hook, giggling in the dark, until the farting begins.

August 29. It feels good to come together in front of Madison Square Garden on the eve of the Republican National Convention. It is so squalid hot the only shade we get is when the zeppelin drifts overhead. We break up and go

back to her apartment to watch the rest of the demonstration on television.

It's one reason [the War, the New World Order] she says she's glad to be on

her way out. [That's a low point.] She was almost see-through; she sat in the half-

dark sort of self-cancellating.

A crowd/ Will gather, and not know it walks the very street

Whereon a thing once walked that seemed a burning cloud.

Whose ghost that is. Steals across the room in alcoholic light. Hers. Not the

specter of her favorite she-cat. The one that often hauled socks from the laundry

by their scruff taking them for her drowned litter. The men's socks, when damp,

the right measure and weight. Since the cat was color-blind, being cat, it didn't

matter if they were all black, the socks, that is.

+ + +

So they drove my friend V out of her home. They drove her out of the

town. They drove her out of the state. Until they burned up her car, she drove herself. Burned her car right next to the police station. She had just begun to

drive, I mean she just learned to drive and she had many miles to go. Then

whoa, Gentle Reader, no more car. The white man burned that MF to the struts.

The governor's bodyguard, Jim, or was he a trooper or was he a trooper whose

trooper duties were to safeguard the governor. Anyway he drove her to the state

line. Drove her across the bridge to Memphis. One thing he knew. He didn't

want her getting killed in Arkansas. The governor didn't want that and the

bodyguard didn't want that. After all he was the one driving, he would likely as

not be killed alongside her. His job was to protect and to serve. It wasn't part of

his plan for her to get killed on his watch. She said he dropped her off at a cafe

on the other side. Under the bridge. I don't know what was there then. That

whole area has turned. Condos and fine houses line the bluff overseeing the big

brown working river.

Some would say she was in full pursuit of her ruin

Some would call it her pathetic adventure

I would say you did not understand the magnitude of her longing

I say where was the suitor to her senescence

Another disaffiliated member of her tribe

I say do we have to go through this every time/ This shunning thing

Any simple problem can be made insoluble

Such as how to share an Elberta with the fuzz still on it

Crickets in the house are good/ A crow is a bad sign

Empty rooms love the dark

The key to tranquillity is equal opportunity

When the siren sounds

It's time for our curfew

Old moon a wrecking ball

The town under demolition from within

Color provides a structure, albeit soul-sucking

The woods were felled by Chicago Mills

An Arkansas arc is not a rainbow

But an iron bridge over troubled waters

+ + +

It was hotter then. It was darker. No sir, it was whiter. Just pick up a paper.

You would never suspect 66% of the population was invisible. You would

never even suspect any of its people were nonwhite until an elusive Negro was

arrested in Chicago or the schedule for the annual Negro Fair was published or

a popular Negro social studies teacher was fired for an insubordinate letter to

the superintendent and a spontaneous rebellion sprang up in a Negro classroom

in the form of flying chairs and raggedy books and a pop bottle thrown at a light

fixture, and then, the lists of long long suffered degradations backed up and

overflowed:

Parades without permits/ Boycotted stores

Funeral home turned into a Freedom Center

Kids arrested en masse and put in a swimming pool

V died during Operation Enduring Freedom

A bottle a day, she got annihilated/ Two packs a day

Always preoccupied with last things/ Always a touch eschatological

Always took a little tabula rasa with her caffeine

When I asked the neighbor if she knew the woman who lived there in 1969/

Oh yes she said/ She knew her

She didn't trust me and I didn't trust her

I don't blame her though/ Everything

was so confusing/ She stayed to herself

She was overwhelmed/ That poor woman...

She was right/ We were wrong

VINDICATION

They've got souls/ Just like you and me

INTERPOSITION AND NULLIFICATION

The marchers are approaching the town of Hazen

where not so long ago an earth scraper turned up

a mastodon skull and a tusk on the old military road

In Big Tree: People are turning in

Only sure thing were the prices:

Grown-ups know the cost of a head of lettuce,

a fryer, a package of thighs; a $500 bag of seed

covers about 5 acres; it takes 20 square feet of cotton

for a medium-size blouse; where nothing is planted,

nothing much grows. The dirt is hard-packed.

The trees were gone by the first war. The first to go,

the most marvelous one, the red cypress,

made beautiful instruments. The fields,

not gone, but empty. Cotton turned to soybeans.

Mussels from the river turned to salvage.

Fishing for tires on the silted-up water.

Some are left digging an old bur out of their foot.

Some go up/ Some go down [Big Tree church sign]

A race-free conversation hard to have back then.

Back then, the hotdog wagon doubled as a brothel.

Come again.

DEAR ABBY,

I am 11 years old but I know all the facts of life because I live in a dirty neighborhood. My problem is that in our family we get pregnate quick. My sister got pregnate when she was 16 just by sitting next to a boy in church. Can this be?

DEAR YOUNG MISS,

No, somebody must have moved.

☩ ☩ ☩

People study the dingy chenille clouds for a sign.

People did what they have done.

A town, a time, and a woman who lived there.

And left undone what they ought not to have did.

135

+ + +

I take one more drive across town thinking about the retired welding
teacher easing over that rise seeing the parking lot full of white men. I wonder
if he thought he would die in the jungle [where no Vietcong ever called him
[N-word]] or he would die in front of the bowling alley [without ever having
been inside] or die in the swimming pool [without ever having been in it, except
when drained, and the police had him in their sights]. Or if, because he was a
young man, he would never die. I attach V to my driving-around thoughts.

An object unworthy of love she thought she was.

It was a *cri de coeur.*

Those of our get had given her a *nom de guerre:* V.

A simple act, to join a march against fear

down an old military road.

We were watching an old movie the night

the table started walking toward us

and there was trouble on Division.

She became a disaffiliated member [of her race].

I'm one of them now, she said, upon release

from jail. I am an Invader.

To feel in conjunction with the changes

of my time. The most alive I've ever been.

My body lifted itself from the chair

it walked to where I saw a silent crowd.

To act, just to act. That *is* the glorious thing.

Yet it has come to my attention that a whisper campaign

has been directed against the main character,

an invisible woman. She could have buried her feelings

like power lines; walked around free

and common as the air that bathes the globe or

sued the chickenshits and gone to live in Provence

smelling of Gauloises and café au lait. You have your life

until you use it. You forfeit the only life you know

or go to your grave with the song curdled inside you.

No more damned if you did and damned if you didn't.

Not the mental lethargy in which the days enveloped her

Nor the depleted breasts not the hand that never knew

tenderness nor eyes that glistened

Not the people dragging canvas bags

through the ragged fields

Not the high mean whine of mosquitoes

Not another year of shoe-top cotton

No more white buck shoes for Henry

No peaches this year on the Ridge, and no other elevation

around to coast another mile out of the tank

No eel in L'Anguille

Not the aphrodisiac of crossing over

Not the hole in the muffler circling the house

Not a shot of whiskey before a piece of bread

Not to live anymore as a distended beast

Not the lying-in again

Not the suicide of the goldfish

Not the father's D.T.'s

Not the map of no-name islands in the river

Not the car burning in the parking lot

Not the sound but the shape of the sound

Not the clouds rucked up over the clothesline

The copperhead in the coleus

Not the air hung with malathion

Not the boomerang of bad feelings

Not stacks of poetry, long-playing albums, the visions of Goya and friends

Not to be resuscitated

and absolutely no priests, up on her elbows, the priests confound you

and then they confound you again. They only come clear when you're on your

deathbed. We must speak by the card or equivocation will undo us.

Look into the dark heart and you will see what the dark eats other than

your heart.

The world is not ineluctably finished

though the watchfires have been doused

more walls have come down

more walls are being built

Sound of the future, uncanny how close

to the sound of the old

At Daddy's Eyes

"Pusherman" still on the jukebox

Everybody's past redacted

✝ ✝ ✝

What to say

to the woman given a folded flag who could not sit

and order a soda in the drugstore

to the druggist who pulled the stools out by the roots

still open for business

to the man, living in Reno now, retired, who was arrested

wrongly, charged, tried, convicted, sentenced.

Picked him up one summer evening when he was on his bicycle making

deliveries for the drugstore.

Then they let him out one night. Drove him home. Told him to go. Just go.

His family collected cash. His mother made food for the journey.

He took a bus to California. Didn't know a living soul.

People were wearing purple pants.

Or the man and his sons,

one son already a veteran, beaten by men from all the farms around. They were waiting for them outside the jailhouse.

They turned off the jailhouse lights and let them loose.

He knew every one of them. He fixed flats for the farms. So he knew every blasted one of them.

His sons took off, one jumped from an overpass.

The father beaten so badly he lost an eye. He was given hot coffee at the hospital. A nurse said, If anyone comes in you can't name, you throw this coffee at them. Anyone.

Your people will be here in no time. You have to go to Memphis.

What to say

to the kids, now scattered, on social security, passed out of this life, or

looking after parents, grandchildren; still working a dead-end job

who were arrested, taken in school buses, then in sealed trucks and put in

the drained pool.

Kids. Sealed trucks. Put in a cement hole. In the ground.

Held at gunpoint for three days. Parents half out of their minds.

It's paved over now. A parking lot. But the pump house isn't gone. Just

overgrown.

I had my friend photograph the pump house, its ghost anyway.

The photographer sees a snake and scrambles up the bank with her tripod.

MR. EASTER: Probably a rat snake.

I'm about like you though about a snake. All these years on the river I only
saw a poison one about three times.

The wife was afraid of spiders, but she'd skin the snakes people would
bring her for a hatband, belts, and whatnot. I'd say, Take that out on the porch. I
don't want a thing to do with them.

When the wife was alive, she kept it beautiful. She loved flowers. I don't do
nothing now but fish. Used to dive for mussels then salvage.

Later the same day we met a city worker [retired] who said he once killed
a cottonmouth on the streets, sold it to a restaurant owner for a dollar, who
skinned, filleted, and served it back to him on a platter.

Later, the same evening, we met a bartender who told us only four people
in history sweat blood and they were all women. It is a place flowing over with
its peculiar feeling.

✝ ✝ ✝

For me

it has always been a series of doors:

if one is opened precipitously a figure is caught bolting from bed

if another, a small table, a list of demands on school paper

if another, a child on the linoleum, saying she wants a white doll

a woman sitting on a bed, holding a folded flag

a shelf of trophies behind her head

an ironing board, bottle of bourbon on the end

sewing machine on a porch

To walk down the road without fear

To sit in a booth and order a sweet soft drink

To work at the front desk

To be referred to as Gentleman

To swim in the pool

To sit in the front row and watch *Run Wild, Run Free* [next week: *Death of a Gunfighter*]

To make your way to the end of the day with both eyes in your head

Nothing is not integral

You want to illumine what you see

Fear reflected off an upturned face

Those walnuts turning black in the grass

It is a relatively stable world

Gentle Reader

But beyond that door

It defies description

I am standing in a sluggish line at the Memphis airport. It is too early. A little girl in a pink sweat suit with tawny corkscrew curls stands behind me. I wish you would just shut up, she says to the stuffed bear she holds. Her mother and I exchange holy-moly looks. I sway between standing and falling. I am flashing the black paintings [before they were transferred onto canvas], and a cock called Helmet, sweet baby JC, a frowsy bush of sweet-betsy, and an old activist with the sobriquet Sweet Willie Wine; there are endless rows of cotton and never enough shade or cool cool water, and rivers silting up and slowing to a standstill, daytime bourbon drinkers, smelly shirts and scrap dogs, clouds of malathion and moccasins in the storm cellar, mussels as big as dinner dishes, a land of lay-offs and morbid obesity, sharp-tongued undertakers, don't-pick-up-hitchhikers correction-facility signs, gentlemen who could not be called gentlemen without it coming back on them, women who could never be called ma'am, rusted iron bridges, towheads, do-rags, tired out schoolbooks, kids put in a drained pool, a pool buried and paved over, brothers scared shitless jumping off an overpass to get away from armed, malevolent men, brothers hiding under the preacher's pickup, blackbirds flashing their red shoulders, speckled bowling balls, segregation after death, and how the death of reason produces monsters.

The Civil Rights Movement has been not only dutifully but beautifully documented, and I am indebted to the brace of books that helped inform my own footnote to the struggle.

Allen, James, and Hilton Als, Congressman John Lewis, and Leon F. Litwack. *Without Sanctuary.* Twin Palms Publishers, 2000. [A devastating photographic document of lynchings.]

Beifuss, Joan Turner. *At the River I Stand.* B&W Books, 1985. [This is the definitive day-by-day account of the Memphis sanitation workers strike. It is a guaranteed-money-back page-turner.]

Branch, Taylor. *Parting the Waters: America in the King Years 1954– 63.* Simon and Schuster, 1988.

——. *Pillar of Fire: America in the King Years 1963–65.* Simon and Schuster, 1998.

——. *At Canaan's Edge: America in the King Years 1965–68.* Simon and Schuster, 2006.
[I mean, somebody say, Amen.]

Capers, Gerald M., Jr. *The Biography of a River Town, Memphis: Its Heroic Age.* Reprint of second edition by Lightning Source for Burke's Bookstore, 2003.

Collins, Martha. *Blue Front: a poem.* Graywolf Press, 2006. [An affecting book-length lyric of a lynching to which her father could have been a very young witness.]

Douglass, Frederick. *Narrative of the Life of Frederick Douglass, an American Slave, Written by Himself.* Signet Paperback, 1968. [Masterly.]

Dray, Philip. *At the Hands of Persons Unknown: The Lynching of Black America.* Modern Library Paperback, 2003. [A devastating textual account of lynchings in America.]

DuBois, W.E.B. *The Negro.* Dover Publications, 2001.

Ellison, Ralph. *Invisible Man.* Modern Library, 1994.

Estes, Steve. *I Am a Man! Race, Manhood, and the Civil Rights Movement.* University of North Carolina Press, 2005.

Gordon, Robert. *It Came from Memphis.* Faber and Faber, 1995. [This book rocks. Memphis deserves a dozen chroniclers of its very own sound.]

Jones, Patricia Spears. *The Weather That Kills* [poems]. Coffee House Press, 1995. [Who was there, among a handful of black students entering the formerly all-white high school the first year of Choice.]

Kennedy, Randall. *Nigger: The Strange Career of a Troublesome Word.* Pantheon Books, 2002. [With a nod in the title to C. Vann Woodward, this book unearths the whole sordid history of the N-word.]

King, Martin Luther, Jr. *Stride Toward Freedom.* Harper and Row, 1958.

——. *Why We Can't Wait.* Signet Classic, 2000.

——. *I Have a Dream: Writings and Speeches That Changed the World.* Edited by James M. Washington. Harper San Francisco, 1992.

——. *A Call to Conscience: The Landmark Speeches of Dr. Martin Luther King, Jr.* Edited by Clayborne Carson and Kris Shepard. Warner Books, 2001.
[When people say so-and-so is a poet when so-and-so is actually a lyricist or a fashion designer or a dog whisperer or a preacher, it sets my tail on fire, but the Reverend, by any lights, was a poet.]

Lancaster, Bob. *The Jungles of Arkansas: A Personal History of the Wonder State.* University of Arkansas Press, 1989. [I am very attached to this smart-mouthed journalist's tucked-up chronicle of the state.]

Rodgers, Clyde Allen. *Lives of Quiet Desperation.* PublishAmerica, 2004. [Novel by a white sharecropper's son whose fictitious Uncle Sal said flatly of his native Arkansas Delta, "It is an ugly country, and it gives me a headache... the mosquitoes are bloodthirsty and bold. I am too old to contend, even with a bug."]

Roy, Beth. *Bitters in the Honey: Tales of Hope and Disappointment across Divides of Race and Time.* University of Arkansas, 1999. [An independent scholar's crucial, absorbing account of Little Rock's infamous year.]

Stockley, Grif. *Blood in Their Eyes: The Elaine Race Massacres of 1919.* University of Arkansas Press, 2001. [Not enough has been written about this unforgivable bloodletting. Stockley's book begins the exhumation.]

Woodruff, Nan Elizabeth. *American Congo: The African American Freedom Struggle in the Delta.* Harvard University Press, 2003. [Hallelujah. She nailed it.]

Woodward, C. Vann. *The Strange Career of Jim Crow.* Reprint of third revised edition, Oxford University Press, 2002. [Sometimes referred to as the Dean of Southern History. Fluid/solid from his earliest writings. Pounds.]

The Memphis *Commercial Appeal,* the *Arkansas Gazette,* and the *Daily Times-Herald* were copiously consulted.

Although I am well aware of the limited reach of an account such as this, I was chary of naming people outright. To begin with, I took the usual writerly liberties to make a go of it. Furthermore, my notes were less than perfect. Weighing heavily on the heart of my reckoning, the town yet seems to tremble. It may tremble in part because of the New Madrid Seismic Zone that underlies the terrain, but in sight of a few casual conversations, it became apparent that emotions reignite in that locale, concerning those days, with a destructive and nearly centrifugal force. Even so, I must thank the individuals who shared their clippings, yearbooks, and letters, and most especially, the memories summoned and branded into their histories.

This is meant as a tribute to Margaret Kaelin McHugh. Our gaggle of unsolicited student acolytes began to call her "V" when she was reading Pynchon while our heads were still rooting among the novels she swallowed whole as a solitary child. Everyone should be favored to know one person of courage [at a critical moment] and genius [of accident and design], though that person arrives with all the flaws and fiends that vex the rest of us, sometimes in disproportionate abundance.

I would like to dedicate this to Mary Pat, her oldest child, for whom V bought a perpetual lottery ticket using the dates of MP's birth, the anticipated winnings from which have long been earmarked by MP to buy a certain Victorian hotel in Coronado, Colorado.

And to the Man Imported from Memphis, Lance Watson, aka Sweet Willie Wine, aka Suhkara Yahweh, a miscreant turned lifelong activist in the wake of the assassination of MLK. Raised by an uncle and aunt. Suhkara's aunt worked as a domestic for Judge Bailey Brown, who less than an hour before King's "sojourn on earth went blank" [Taylor Branch], lifted the restraining order against the scheduled march of the sanitation workers. Suhkara's great-grandfather was Benjamin F. Booth, who practiced law in Memphis for 50-plus years and in 1905 challenged Tennessee's law authorizing the segregation of blacks and whites on streetcars. [Ever forward, never backwards, Suhkara.]

I would also like to thank V's other children: Hoagie, Freddie, Jessie, Sam, Katie, and Robert David, who bore the stigma of being the offspring of one unflinchingly unappeasable woman.
And Stephen.

Also:
Jane Pfeiffer and Beverly Craddock, friends of V's from St. Francis of Assisi primary school through the

Sacred Heart years, who vividly recalled: V smoking in
the playhouse, writing anonymous letters [with gloves
on] to the principal, and V always taking the fall for any
mischief they committed together. How she was always
at the library, always on the list for books she shouldn't
have. One friend recalled how thrilled V was when
her German grandfather took her to see *The Picture of
Dorian Gray*. Both women spoke of the emotional cold-
ness and strictness of the family home in which the an-
swer to most petitions and desires was a foregone N-O.
BC said, ask her to go anywhere, and the answer was,
No, I can't I have to listen to the opera today. No, I have
to memorize poetry. She would give you the shirt off her
back, BC said of her friend. So brilliant that her friends
often claimed she educated them.

Her ex-husband, Joe, who though a nonparticipant
in its conflicts, suffered the cruel will of his adopted
Delta town. He too endured the bind of their incongru-
ous marriage. He remained dispiritingly marked by the
compromising challenge of his wife's actions.

Marilyn Hohmann, their mothers being sisters,
their fathers being brothers, making them, bilateral
parallel cousins? [Something like that.] Who expressed
her deep love and admiration for her cousin. Among
her many memories, she and V would be sitting on the
stairs, making too much noise, her father would call
her up whereupon her punishment would be to read
Elizabeth Barrett Browning to him.

The late Wordan Miller, the McHugh family hired

hand, who lived with them on the farm, kept a pet alliga-
tor in a cement pool he built for it. V's closest [in truth,
her sole] companion on the farm.

Freddie Lou McDaniel, a neighbor and beloved
friend of V's for many years, the years when they
laughed like people were meant to laugh, and with
whom she played bridge when they were too pregnant
to reach the table. Monica Mitchell, also hugely preg-
nant at the bridge table [though I was never able to
make contact with her].

My friends, former residents and, in varying
degrees, natural-born aliens of their town: Cecelia
Grobmyer, a neighbor child during those years, who said
of V, "She was my show-and-tell," the inimitable Nan
Montgomery Signorelli, and the irrepressible Barbara
Barg, who said so movingly of our much-missed friend,
"She taught me how to live; now she has taught me how
to die."

Chris Thomas Ellis, of Memphis [until California fi-
nally cast him in parts that exposed only a scintilla of his
burning mind], whose head cracked along the exact same
lines as hers. Exactly along the same lines.

MLN, whom I did not meet, but according to V's
former husband—she put out the word to State Trooper
Dwight Galloway assigned to the March Against Fear
that he had better not let any harm come to a hair on
V's head. This was sticking-up-for-behind-the-scenes of
which there was precious little to be had from any other
white citizens and absolutely sum zero to be tallied on
the scene.

Ruthie Mae Cochran West, among the kids
never allowed to go near the pool until transported
there under arrest; who was told by Sheriff Clarence
Montgomery they were to be taken to the woods and
killed. Who had no idea where they were being taken;
whose parents did not know where they were held.
Ms. West's brothers Theo, Leo, Frank Jr., George, and
Curtis, who jumped from the long-torn-down overpass
from which there were once lynchings [five officially
confirmed in the town]. And her father, Frank Cochran
Sr., who lost an eye to a beating by some seventy men
he knew by name; then was he fired from his longtime
job by dint of that same knowledge. Honor due also to
Tarlee Babbs, grandmother of RMCW, who brought dig-
nity and stability to everyone in her charge.

Pat Flanagan, who knows the town cold, its best
fishing holes and hunting grounds, its public hous-
ing and fine homes, its corrupt officials, its anonymous
night riders.

Willie Hicks, who works the night shift; who with
his wife takes care of his 94-year-old father; who was
there, who knows.

Edna Lockhart, who was there, but was too weary,
too busy, and possibly too leery to have the conversa-
tion; who was reported to have been taken to Mississippi
in the dogcatcher's wagon to be put in detention.

John Henry Watson, who joined a Canadian football
league after graduating in 1963, no such opportunities
available to him in his native land.

Effie Y. Clay, director of a funeral home, who

came by her backbone honestly, daughter of Florence Katherine Clay, who gave sanctuary to the civil rights meetings in the home when she was its proprietor, and posted bond for the Man Imported from Memphis.

Charlene Sykes, retired teacher and social worker, who stood all night holding to the bars after an un-provoked arrest by a widely loathed sheriff. She was younger then she said, and could stand long hours, which she chose over sitting on a jailhouse cot.

Her daughter, Shirley S. Ingram, whom Mrs. Sykes roused from a peaceful summer sleep to talk to me on another line. Who grew up with the Klan. "Everyone knew who was Klan, who was not Klan."

The late Odessa Bradley, a teacher who stood tall by her kids, and lived just long enough to see the 1969 [Arkansas] March Against Fear observed with pride. This march, led by Sweet Willie Wine, stepped off in West Memphis and plodded the hot two-lane highway to Little Rock [not to be confused with its predecessor, the March Against Fear begun June 5, 1966, by James Meredith, which stepped off from the Peabody Hotel in Memphis and ended some 15,000 strong in Jackson, June 26, despite Meredith having been wounded almost at the outset].

Donnie Bell, who was a magnet and foil in those days for the wild side of V, and who claimed his family, "all country club people," condemned him to death for being her friend.

I also recall quoting or paraphrasing Sir Isaac Newton, Edna St. Vincent Millay, Francis Ford Coppola,

Liam Clancy, Harry Mattison, Allen Ginsberg, Walt
Whitman, and who else, William Butler Yeats, of course,
V's first true love.

Shirley Harvell, a force unto herself, who spear-
headed a commemoration of the 1969 March Against
Fear twenty-five years later and provided me with the
sole audio recording of my late friend, made from a tele-
phone interview in preparation for that event.

Patricia Spears Jones, poet of New York, who goes
home to see family and is hauntingly struck by the emp-
tiness of the vast fields that were populous with pickers
young and old when she was coming up. Who testified
to her family's "ordinary courage" in *The Weather That
Kills.* She wrote that I was going to have a very diffi-
cult time there. It is a town with as many secrets as Los
Angeles, and many of the major players are now in their
graves. Her sister Gwendolyn F. Jones, who was in sixth
grade when the high school erupted; whose mother was
on the spot to get her baby girl out of harm's way. Her
brother, Sheriff William C. Spears of Memphis, who
stuck to his drums in high school just as his sister stuck
to her studies.

Dolores F. Morelon, who provided me with the
names and numbers of individuals put in the swimming
pool; who lived behind the antenna place, as she de-
scribed the appliance sales and repair business owned by
V's former husband.

James Johnson, Vietnam veteran, who came back
with a purple heart to find his town in a racist tem-
pest—a white mob ready and willing to spit on a

returning black soldier. Whose kids were "all military." Whose oldest son was shot and killed by a Memphis police officer, also African American. People are people, he said. He came back, he said, to Jesus, the only way.

M. Lowe, known as Tex, the SNCC worker [who escaped eastern Arkansas by the hair of his chinny chin chin].

Tom Rountree, veterinarian, whose father, a postman and minister of gentle disposition, took his son to the movies the night the town erupted; the first spool was no sooner reeling than it was brought to a smoky halt.

Rosie Stewart, owner of the Blue Flame, who fed and sheltered the group that dubbed themselves the Invaders, but who held no illusions about their personal conduct.

Evans Seawood, retired police captain, who could identify the man in the photo who found himself in possession of damning audiotapes of interrogations that did not make their way to the county museum as promised.

Harvey Hanna, who ran the county museum with the voluntary assistance of his wife, Carolyn, preserving as much of the town's history as it seemed collectively willing to contribute to the record.

H. Ford Hunt, whom I happened to meet in front of Oscar's; who was arrested and put in the pool; whose mother told her not to get in that line, not to even think about getting in that line, that she would not come see her in jail, though later HFH learned that her mother had in fact tried to see her.

Story L. Matkin-Rawn, whose doctoral thesis historicizes the recent struggle for human rights in the Arkansas Delta.

James T. Easter, who lives on the bank of the river. Who watched the river he had fished all his life turn from a place to haul mussels to a dredging site for big tires; and spoke so kindly of his late wife who could skin snakes and tend flowers with equal ease.

Joe Williams, retired welding teacher, who met me at Colonel Sanders for syrupy soft drinks and ranging conversation. Who was in the second wave of marchers who were put in the drained pool; who on the eve of military induction, with his friends James Nesbitt and Robert Smith, known as Toad, determined to integrate the bowling alley. Soon after, it burned. Who moved to integrate the drugstore. Soon after, the booths and stools were yanked out. His boss at T-C who stood up for him once when a white customer started abusing him while his broom stirred up a little dust.

L.C. Poole [brother of Joe Williams] of Las Vegas; to whom a great injustice was done.

Sue Saunders or Sanders, whom I was never able to locate, the redheaded *Gazette* stringer whispered to have been a federal agent.

Charlene Warren, retired teacher, who lent her scarce-as-hen's-teeth 1967 LHS yearbook to the town museum.

Arlisa Price and Carolyn Sanders, of the public library, helpful in the patient, hands-on practice of librarians.

John Greeley and Marcos Rivero, who put up a plaque in V's memory on the barren pear outside her apartment in Hell's Kitchen.

Deborah Luster, who drove and flew up several times from New Orleans to meet me in the Arkansas Delta to provide me with the evidentiary image, at a time when her own life was much distressed.

The late Reverend Vernon Johns, rousing pastor of Dexter Avenue Baptist Church, Montgomery, Alabama, prior to MLK, from whom I cribbed the title of one of his famous sermons, "Segregation After Death."

C.D. WRIGHT was born in the Arkansas Ozarks, almost exclusively white at that time [except for a pocket of African American hill people in the university town of Fayetteville, and a lone hermit in Eureka Springs, Richard Banks]. Harrison, the town in which Wright mostly grew up, carried out two violent cleansings, in 1905 and 1909. Until very recent years it remained a sundown town. In 2003 a small collection of white citizens in Harrison initiated a recognition and reconciliation task force focused on opposing all forms, signs, and traces of racism. Their efforts included a bus trip from the Ozarks to an African Methodist Episcopal church routed from Harrison a hundred years earlier that had reestablished itself in the Arkansas Delta. The West Helena church had just launched a campaign to raise funds for repairs. The parish warmly received the Harrison delegation's offer of in-kind support. One church member commented, "It's like a situation where a bone is broken. When healing is complete, the bone is stronger at that break than it was before the injury." Even if the science is iffy, the symbolism wavers not.

AN OLD CLASSMATE OF WRIGHT's: "It's mostly outsiders, the task force."

Knights of the Ku Klux Klan, P.O. Box 2222, is currently headquartered in Zinc, near Harrison.

I want people of twenty seven languages walking back and
    forth saying to one
another hello brother how's the fishing
and when they reach their destination I don't want them
    to forget if it was bad

Since 1972, Copper Canyon Press has fostered the work of emerging, established, and world-renowned poets for an expanding audience. The Press thrives with the generous patronage of readers, writers, booksellers, librarians, teachers, students, and funders — everyone who shares the belief that poetry is vital to language and living.

Copper Canyon Press gratefully acknowledges board member

JIM WICKWIRE

in honor of his many years of service to poetry and independent publishing.

Lannan

NATIONAL
ENDOWMENT
FOR THE ARTS

Major support has been provided by:

Amazon.com

Anonymous

Beroz Ferrell & The Point, LLC

Golden Lasso, LLC

Lannan Foundation

Rhoady and Jeanne Marie Lee

National Endowment for the Arts

Cynthia Lovelace Sears and Frank Buxton

William and Ruth True

Washington State Arts Commission

Charles and Barbara Wright

To learn more about underwriting
Copper Canyon Press titles, please call
360-385-4925 x103

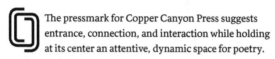 The pressmark for Copper Canyon Press suggests
entrance, connection, and interaction while holding
at its center an attentive, dynamic space for poetry.

This book is set in Parable, designed for digital composition by
Christopher Burke in 2002. Titles are set in Helvetica Neue. Book
design and composition by Valerie Brewster, Scribe Typography.

Printed in the USA
CPSIA information can be obtained
at www.ICGtesting.com
JSHW060043150824
68134JS00028B/2619

9 781556 593888